SHADOWS OF WAR

SHADOWS OF WAR

Dr. William A. Allen

SHADOWS OF WAR

First Printing 2020

ISBN: 9798636881759

This memoir is dedicated to five people who greatly impacted my life. Eunice rarely caught a break and lived her life in poverty. Ralph could never escape the long shadows of the Second World War. Iona's mistake was to marry a man who suffered from PTSD. They all deserved better.

It is also dedicated to Uncle Leon whose generosity lessened the burden on our family and who changed the course of my life.

And finally, to Dorothy, who has shared the best fifty seven years of my life.

ACKNOWLEDGMENTS

The author wishes to acknowledge and thank the people who helped see the book through to completion.

Dr. Ken Langeland first suggested that I write the story and helped find many of the records of the Allen family ancestors.

Mrs. Leatha Bourne proved to be a treasure of historical information about the King side of my family and filled in additional records about the Allens. Leatha provided some of the pictures in the early chapters.

Mrs. Dorothy Allen added many suggestions about the content to be shared.

Dr. Jim Thomas assisted with improving old photographs and he and his wife Beth critically reviewed the manuscript before it was published.

All five have spent countless hours editing the manuscript, for which I am deeply grateful.

PROLOGUE

A memoir is always a construction of memories and stories. Both are important, but each is unique. Memories are like water. They can be as soothing as a gentle stream on a hot day or they can drown you in a flood of emotion as dangerous as an ocean in a hurricane. They are part of your entire being because you were participant and witness to them. They lie deep in your soul. Like water over porous stone they seep into your subconscious and return to the surface when you least expect them. They are always with you.

Stories are more like stones in a wall. They are second hand accounts of events, places and people that we learn of through the telling of the account by third persons. The events may be completely or partially true based on how many times the wall has been repaired. To be entirely accurate we must place each stone in its proper place. Even then, you can never be sure of the stories accuracy or of a wall's strength because you were not there when it was being built.

Both memories and stories shape our values and expectations, and give us guideposts to order our lives. They give us structure and pleasure or regret. They change with their recounting because all memories and stories are nuanced by time and our perception of the events that shaped them. All of our memories are molded and etched deep into our subconscious, so they change little. The stories are nearer the surface and more easily fade. With each retelling, details are lost and added, and may in the end, be more the way we remember them than the way they happened. The following pages contain some of my memories and stories. The stories are pieced together from those that as a young child I heard from my mother and other family members. At best they are an interpretation of what I remember. The memories are real.

This is my story of growing up in rural Florida in a time of war and peace, both domestic and foreign, and of the life that followed.

PART ONE

PEACE, WAR, FAMILY, HARD TIMES, AND MY MEMORY OF TOADS

CHAPTER ONE

THE HOMECOMING

In February 1946 my father, Private First Class Ralph Carl Allen, arrived unannounced from World War II. He had fought in the Philippine battle for Luzon and like thousands of young men, had seen the carnage of that bloody war. He was a handsome man, five feet eleven inches tall, lean, muscular, and smartly dressed in his infantryman's uniform. The War Department had made a major push to get the troops home by Christmas but others who had served longer were given preference for return to the states. His time in the jungle and the travel home were etched on his face. My mother, Eunice (King) Allen, my older brother Leon and I had not seen him since his departure in October 1944, and although Mom had written him faithfully for the duration of his absence, he had seldom responded. We did not know then of the depth of hell into which he had descended or of the long shadows that memories of the recent past would cast upon him. Nor did we know that our family would be forever changed from that time forward.

There was a party at our house that Saturday night. My mother had invited several of her friends, one of her sisters, and a few soldiers with their girlfriends from the local Army Air Corp training base. Mom worked at the base in the Post Exchange to help make ends meet. Several children in my age group had accompanied their parents and we were thrilled to be allowed to stay up late with the adults. The music from the radio which someone had brought was playing Nat King Cole's

"For Sentimental Reasons" and other tunes of that era, and there was laughter and talk of the better times ahead. The war had ended the previous August with the dropping of the atomic bombs on Nagasaki and Hiroshima and the war-weary people were happy. Some couples danced with the lights low in the living room, others drank beer and talked in little groups. Several women joined my mother in the kitchen helping dispense the snacks that everyone had brought. A washtub was filled with ice, beer and soft drinks. Children played and giggled. The air was heavy with cigarette smoke and the smell of beer. Everyone was having a good time and completely surprised when Dad walked in.

When she spied him, Mom ran over and threw her arms around Dad and they embraced, but his enthusiasm was less than hers. She was near tears with joy and kept hugging him. She asked why he had not written back for more than two months. He was irritated by what he saw and made no effort to hide it. Those who knew him came over to welcome him back home, but he was indifferent.

My nine year old brother, Leon, approached him and Dad leaned down, drew him near and asked him how he was. "I'm fine," he replied. "I am happy you are home Dad. Are you home for good?" Dad replied, "Yes, I'm home. I will not be going back. Not ever."

I watched him from across the room but was shy about approaching him. He left for the war when I was only four and I had not seen him since the day he boarded the train at the station in our small town of Kissimmee. Other smartly dressed young men in military uniform had boarded with him after one final visit home to say goodbye to loved ones. Mothers, fathers, wives, girlfriends, children and friends had gathered at the train station to get a last hug or a handshake, to bid them farewell and Godspeed. Some cried while others waved bravely as the train pulled out of the station. Many just looked at their feet because everyone knew that some would never come back, for such is the nature of war.

When I did come closer he patted me on the head and told me how I had grown. I was now six years old.

Dad had been drinking when he first walked into the room but was not over the edge. After surveying the room, he walked into the kitchen to the galvanized wash tub that contained iced down bottles of beer and soft drinks. Taking a Seven Up he made himself a stiff drink with whiskey from one of the several open bottles that decorated the kitchen table. Other mixed drinks would soon follow. Mom was constantly at his side with her arm around him, offering snacks and introducing him to those whom he did not know. Soldiers asked him for details of his service because some had only served stateside. Dad was in no mood to discuss the war and his drinking was making him become disagreeable. He became more over the edge with each drink, until he finally exploded and ordered everyone out of the house. People quickly gathered their sweaters, coats, half empty snack dishes and left. The party was over. The hell was yet to come.

Dad told Leon and me to go to bed which we promptly did. For the next two hours there was loud arguing as Dad berated Mom for daring to have parties while he was at war in the mud and carnage in jungles far away. He accused her of having parties so that she could be unfaithful. Dad said that he had arrived earlier in the day and had visited with his mother, Ruby, who had written to him about the parties and made accusations of infidelity. Ralph said that others had confirmed the stories of loose living. My mother denied them. When he finally was drunk enough, and could stand to argue and curse her any more, he beat her until he was punched out, then went to bed and passed out.

It was the first time she had ever been assaulted. It would not be the last. Leon and I lay in the bed we shared, and I cried myself to sleep.

CHAPTER TWO

RALPH AND EUNICE

War changes people. Some never come back and are buried on foreign soil. Others survive but have injuries that deform them. They are missing arms or legs and have horrible scars to remind them of their time in hell. Dad had none of these. He arrived home without a scratch. He was physically fit and carried himself well. When sober he had an easy smile and people liked him. Dad's scars were hidden deep in his soul, in places none of us could reach. The memories haunted him, and he relived them again and again. They came more frequently when he drank, and whiskey often made him weep as he recounted his time in battle. Those who cared about him could only listen, with the hope that someday the demons would leave him. They never did.

Dad had not always been this way. In his youth he was popular among those who knew him. He met my mother, Eunice, when they were teenagers and they married soon after.

Mom was the second of seven children born to Hannah and Albert King. Hannah Elizabeth Sophia Palmquist was the third wife of Albert and married him on December 15, 1914, when she was only sixteen years old. Albert was fifty seven. The young bride was said to "have hair the color of a new penny."

Hannah had been born November 11, 1898, in Penn Township, Westmoreland, Pennsylvania, to Swedish Immigrants John Emil Palmquist and Mary Elizabeth Johnson. John had become a naturalized citizen in Pittsburg, Pennsylvania, on April 28, 1883, and they settled in Penn

Township to raise a family. To their great sorrow they lost three small children to a house fire in December 1886 nearly two years before Hannah was born. The Palmquists later moved to Kissimmee and owned property near Albert's farm on Cypress Island.

Albert had grown up in Ohio where he had become a successful bridge builder. There were unconfirmed rumors that he had left the state after killing his second wife's lover, and absconding with the liquid assets of the Medina Bridge Company, that he jointly owned with a partner. He had been born Albert Kingsley Loomis on June 17, 1857, in Weymouth, Ohio, and served in the military under that name. He was an officer in the Spanish-American War and later settled in Kissimmee when veterans were being recruited to help populate the area. Upon moving to Kissimmee he changed his name to Albert L. King, and bought land on what was called Cypress Island to begin farming.

Albert's farm was located on or near what is now the Sunset Point Subdivision. He named his vegetable farm "Gold Medal Farm".

The properties purchase appeared in the January 27, 1911, copy of the Kissimmee Valley Gazette on page 7, column 3,

"Mr. A.L. King, a recent arrival from the North, <u>has purchased from R. O. Meek the old Hirtzel Place across the lake,</u> and has already taken up residence there and is preparing to plant a spring crop."

Albert shared Cypress Island with a Mr. Hirtzel and Mr. Rasmus P. Hansen who also farmed. An April 1, 1911, account of the Orlando Evening Star, reported on Mr. Hansen's crop as follows.

"Five hundred crates of beans.

Mr. R.P. Hansen, who owns Cypress Island, which lies in the lake about one mile from the city dock, and trucks something like twenty five acres of it, is this week engaged in picking for the first

time his five acre-bean field, having twenty five people at work, and when they are through Mr. Hansen will have five hundred crates, which will bring him one thousand dollars, and still the field will be picked three time again before the vines cease bearing. The field will not yield quite as much in the other three pickings as it will in this first one, but those who have seen the crop say that Mr. Hansen will gather at least fifteen hundred crates, which at low figures should net him one dollar and fifty cents a crate -Valley Gazette"

This and other newspaper accounts that follow have been reproduced exactly as printed, including misspellings.

The term Cypress Island is confusing because the property where the King family lived is contiguous with the mainland. High parcels of land that were surrounded by large marshy areas were sometimes called islands. The reporter's account of Cypress Island, suggests the he had not visited Mr. Hansen's farm. The misspelling of "least" is as it appears in the article , and the extremely long conjunctive sentences are accurately reproduced.

A June 20, 1913, article on page 8 of the Kissimmee Valley Gazette read as follows.

"A. L. King Keeps Accurate Account Of Money Received For Crop.

This is no idle dream, boost story or hot air effusion. It's plain, unvarnished truth, and the men are here to verify it.

A. L. King owns a truck garden across the lake immediately alongside the Sugar Belt Railway. This spring he planted a quarter of an acre to tomatoes, and up to this date he has sold $ 227.72 worth of the crop and still has several crates to pick. These tomatoes were bought mostly by Waters & Carson Grocery Co., of this city, who are prepared to verify the figures, and there are hundreds of people who have seen the King tomato patch and will testify that it was not over a quarter of an acre in size.

Mr. King will plant velvet beans on the land in a couple of weeks, and potatoes this fall. The latter crop will net him about $40, which will make at least $275 he will receive this year from that quarter acre."

The expected return was a significant amount of money in 1913. Tailored blouses were being advertised in the same paper for 98 cents as late as May 23, 1915.

On September 1, 1931, when Mom was thirteen years old, her mother, Hannah, died at age thirty two. Hannah passed away from complications of a weak heart, a hardscrabble life and frequent child birth. When Hannah died, she left behind seven children. Mom's brother Ralph was almost 16 years old, Mom (Eunice) 13, Ruth 11, Charles 9, Betty 6, Earl 3, and Virginia 18 months. Albert died ten years later but managed to care for all seven of his children on a ten-acre truck farm on Cypress Island, and later on a much smaller plot of land at what is now the intersection of Altman and Neptune Roads. Albert and Hannah had moved from Cypress Island to the new house about 1928, three years before Hannah died.

In those days, there was no welfare assistance in Kissimmee, a cattle town that Carmy Johnson once said had too many saloons and too few churches. Although their father was still alive, Eunice and Ruth assumed additional responsibility for the care of the younger children. Their father, Albert, tended the truck farm, cooked their meals and watched them grow up. Uncle Earl later confided to my cousin, Leatha King Bourne, that his father Albert must have been a good cook because they all lived!

Mom said that the old man was stingy, and Uncle Earl related that daily beatings for the boys were standard fare.

Now becoming adults, the three older children began their own lives. Ralph King married Mary Moore, September 25, 1933, and Eunice and Ruth, soon after took husbands. All three of them married when they were 17 years old.

Eunice married Dad on April 9, 1935. Within a year, her younger sister Ruth married Dad's older brother Cliff. They all started married life full of youthful energy and hope for the future. It was the middle of the Great Depression. Times were hard.

Ralph Carl and Eunice Marie (King) Allen
Photograph courtesy of Leatha Bourne

My father, Ralph, was the fourth of possibly six children born to his mother Ruby Estelle (Acree) Allen. The first four, W.C., Clifton, Iris and Ralph were fathered by my grandfather William Harvel Allen. Stories persisted that Will and Ruby had another daughter that died from a rattlesnake bite when she was three years old. Dad's half-brother, Dick Perfitt, was the youngest of Ruby's children, born after her marriage to her second husband Earl Richard Perfitt.

Ruby and Will divorced when Dad was young and the three oldest boys later spent time living with my great-uncle Leon Vernon Allen and his mother, Nancy Jane (Nipper) Allen. "Uncle Leon" as we all called him was the younger brother of my grandfather, William Harvel Allen.

Grandpa Will and Grandma Ruby were both native-born Floridians, as were most of my kin. Ruby could trace her family back to John Lanier, an early Florida Cattle King, and an uncle by marriage, Alfred Sidney Campbell who was born before Florida became a state on March 3, 1845. The towns of Campbell and Lake Alfred are named after the Campbells. Ruby's father, Steve Acree, served two terms as County Commissioner and one term as State Representative.

Grandpa Will and Uncle Leon's family was less prominent. Their father, William Allen, was born in March 1850, in Louisiana and migrated in the 1800's to Florida from Alabama, where family lore said that he had killed a man and decided to not wait to see how the trial turned out.

Once married, Mom and Dad rented a tiny unpainted house on Gilbert Street on the outskirts of Kissimmee. When I was a teenager, an uncle pointed out the shot-gun house to me and I was surprised at how small it was.

Like millions of others during the depression, life was difficult for the newly-weds. Jobs were hard to find, money was scarce, and there was a baby on the way. My brother, Leon, was born on March 1, 1936.

Dad worked manual labor for the WPA. President Franklin D. Roosevelt had signed the Emergency Relief Appropriations Act creating the Works Progress Administration on April 8, 1935. Mom said that he made a dollar a day and was thankful for the work. Because Florida was flood prone, the government employed hundreds of local men to dig drainage ditches with shovels in President Roosevelt's work recovery projects. At night he went to trade school and learned to be an electrician.

I came along on June 15, 1939. That same year Dad bought four lots in the Magnolia Park section of St. Cloud for taxes due to local government, presumably to build a house at some future time. They never did.

Then on September 1, 1939, Hitler's Luftwaffe flew over Wieluń, Poland and bombed and strafed the town at 4:40 a.m. The town had no apparent military value but it was Hitler's first victim in the deadliest war in human history. Seventy million people would die before the conflict ended. In time, America would be drawn into the conflict, but for the next two years, people went about their lives thinking that this was Europe's problem.

In February 1942, just before he turned twenty, Charles assumed guardianship of the three younger children, Betty, Earl and Virginia. The following week, Charles married and he shouldered the responsibility until guardianship for Earl and Virginia was transferred to Ruth on November 12, 1943. At the time of the transfer Ruth's second husband Henry Sullivan was away in the Army. Betty was 17 years old and no longer a child. She had married on April 5, 1943 and was living with her husband James Harrah. Although Ruth was Earl and Virginia's legal guardian, Mom said that Virginia and Earl also spent time with her and Dad.

A year earlier, in February 1941, Earl was severely injured on his way to school when struck by a car several days before his father, Albert died on February 16. Family lore suggested that Earl may not have been going to school but instead was leaving home because of the beatings by his father.

Albert L. King shortly before his death in 1941 at age 83.
Photograph courtesy of Leatha Bourne.

Earl was only thirteen years old. His injuries were extensive. The impact had cracked his skull and his brain was exposed. The doctor on duty when he was admitted to the hospital, said that there was no hope for survival. It was reported that Dad threatened the doctor to force him to try to save Earl's life. Dad would later joke that with most people you could not tell if they had a brain, but there was no doubt that Earl had one.

Earl did survive, but spent time in hospitals in Kissimmee and Orlando before being admitted to Harry-Anna Crippled Children's Hospital in Umatilla. He later said that he was still in the hospital on Halloween, October 31, 1941. Pearl Harbor was only a few weeks away.

Although Earl quit school when he was 13 years old, he later earned his GED when in his seventies. Growing up he lived with a number of people around Limit Street.

Once he recovered, Uncle Earl sometimes visited, staying over to talk with Mom or to eat a meal. He and Mom were close, and she was always happy when he showed up. He came more often to check on us when Dad was in the Pacific. In my grade school years I would see him around town but never really knew him well. When he was 18 years old, he said that he lived for a time with Tavy Johnson on Limit Street. Earl walked with a limp, the result of the accident in 1941. I lost track of him for ten years until he showed up at my home in Indian Rocks Beach one Sunday morning in 1965. We talked, ate lunch, discussed our lives and he left. I never saw him again.

After our family expanded, Mom and Dad rented a frame house at the city limits of Kissimmee. The tin-roofed house was painted white. It had a living room, two bedrooms, dining room, a kitchen and a large front porch. The amenities included an outdoor hand pump for drawing water for drinking, cooking, bathing and washing clothes. Kerosene lamps supplied our lighting. An outhouse was located about one hundred feet behind the house but required that you go through a large fenced-in area that the owner of the property earlier had used to keep a milk cow.

There were two small buildings on the property. One of them was a small shed inside the fence and the other building was outside the enclosure. One part of the outside building formed a portion of the fence. Mom used the shed to wash our clothes by hand, using a rub board in a galvanized wash tub. She had a wash pot nearby that she heated with a wood fire to boil our clothes.

The other building was filled with rusty tools, and dozens of stacked boxes filled with nails, screws, door hinges, old spark plugs, and assorted curiosities left by the owner and previous renters. That building was a source of endless mystery to my brother Leon, our cousin Henry Allen, a neighborhood friend Charley Lee, and me

One day when Charley and I were playing in the out-building, we opened a box at the bottom of the pile. After rummaging through its contents for several minutes, Charley saw something strange. It was made of metal, covered with rust, and looked like a small pineapple. I had no idea what it was, but Charley thought that he did. We decided to show it to Mom. Charley picked it up and we headed toward the back door of the house. Mom was in the kitchen and saw us coming from the building. When she saw what we were carrying, she sailed out the door and shouted "Stop! Now listen to me. Charley put that down very carefully. Don't drop it!" Charley did as he was told. Mom then told us to back away from it. It was a hand grenade. The grenade had apparently been stolen from the Army Base at some time in the past and forgotten when the occupants moved on.

Mom did not wait until dad came home. Instead, she dispatched my brother, Leon, to go see if Uncle Leon was home. He was and soon they returned in his cattle truck. Uncle Leon examined the grenade for several minutes without touching it, then said, "I need to bury it." Uncle Leon dug a deep hole in the far back corner of the property. He then gently carried the grenade to the hole he had prepared and placed it at the bottom, before covering it with sand. Afterwards he told Dad that the pin was intact but he did not know whether or not, the grenade was armed and dangerous, or if it had been a training prop.

That weekend Dad went through the entire contents of the boxes in the building to make sure that there were no other items that might harm us.

The front yard of the house was grassed and a large camphor tree shaded the porch and the front bedroom, where my parents slept. In one corner of the yard a large gardenia bush perfumed the air when it bloomed. Mom had never lived so well, and she was happy.

Dad had been pleased to see the fenced-in pen in the back yard. We had a billy goat that he said was left over from when he and Earl had made a cart and bought the goat to pull it. The goat was not fond of this conscription and the cart was soon wrecked beyond repair. Earl later left, but the goat remained. The fenced in area meant that the goat would no longer have to be tethered each day.

The goat was aggressive and when I was just learning to go

unassisted to the outhouse, he would butt me and knock me to the ground. He also butted my brother, but Leon was large enough to withstand his pushing. Mom seemed unconcerned about the goat until she was hit hard enough to lose her balance. The next day Uncle Leon took the goat away and I never saw him again. The goat was not mourned.

Railroad tracks ran beside the house. The trains ferried food and supplies to the Army Airbase about a mile away. Fighter pilots trained at the base and were then sent to the Pacific Theater and over the Atlantic Ocean to fight in the European Theater. The pilots flew low over our house practicing their strafing runs at a large bunker that had been constructed on the base to provide a target. The bunker was a half mile away. To the kids in the neighborhoods they flew over, they were all "Flying Tigers" and we would yell and wave when they passed overhead. The planes flew low enough for us to see the pilots, and to our great joy, some of them would wave back as they approached their target.

When the train passed by a couple of times each week, my brother and I were always there to greet them. The train barely moved, and the men aboard would throw oranges and apples to us from supplies destined for the people stationed at the base. Occasionally, they threw candy, much to our delight.

These were happy days for our whole family. Mom and Dad were in love. It was the best house either one had ever lived in. We saw uncles, aunts and cousins on a regular schedule. With his newly earned license, Dad was working as an electrician and had money to buy their first car. He washed it every weekend.

As soon as it got dark on warm summer evenings, we hunted toads.

CHAPTER THREE

TOAD HUNTING

Two year old Bill Allen

My earliest memories are of hunting toads and playing hide and seek in our front yard. On summer evenings, after we had finished supper and the sun had set over the Chinese cabbage fields beyond the railroad tracks, my father would authorize the great front yard safari. It was almost a nightly ritual and in the mind of three or four year-old boy it rivaled any lion hunt in Africa.

By sundown Dad would have rested up from his day's labor, drank a bottle of cold beer, then washed his hands and face for the evening meal. Supper was always served shortly before sunset to allow the house to cool down from the summer heat. The house stayed uncomfortably warm long after the sun went down in the summer months but everyone adjusted to the heat. None of my family had yet heard of air conditioning.

For me, Mom's meal was often merely a prologue to the evening's entertainment. Nevertheless, Mom's rules were inviolate, and she demanded that my brother and I eat all of the food on our plates before we could be excused. After gobbling down my food, I would wait impatiently for Mom and Dad to finish theirs, to be excused. For some reason Dad was never in a hurry to finish his meal and would make the wait unbearable by talking to Mom while downing a couple of glasses of iced tea before leaving the table. She never seemed to be in a hurry either. I finally concluded that Mom did not like to hunt toads, but I had no idea why.

For anyone unfamiliar with toads, they are easily found through the state of Florida. There are several species in the state but the most common is the Southern Toad which ranges widely over the peninsula. Toads are a terrestrial frog species that hide under plants, logs or other cover, and some species will burrow into loose soil. Southern Toads typically are brown or gray, with short legs and warty skin. Adults are 1.5 to 3 inches long. They eat a variety of insects and are active after darkness falls. The common Southern Toad is safe to handle but when picked up they urinate to dispel predators. This seldom deters small boys.

Unfortunately, an exotic species from Latin America, The Cane Toad, is now displacing the native species. The Cane Toad is not safe to handle because it has toxins in its skin. Pets who try to eat them sometime die from their poison. It is but one of a great many exotic species of plants and animals that unfortunately are changing the landscape of Florida

When darkness fell, Leon and I were released from Mom's ever watchful eye with the admonition, "Don't let them pee on you or you will get warts." I never knew if she really believed that or if she said it out of habit.

Dad then gave each of us a flashlight to better find our quarry and to avoid snakes. Our home was surrounded by unimproved pastureland on three sides. The fields were made up of pine trees, palmettos and most importantly, carpet grass upon which the cattle fed. Such habitats are well known to harbor the eastern diamondback rattlesnake and like most predators they move around in search of prey. Although we found them on the property, we never encountered one during our nightly activities.

Once we had located our quarry, and triumphantly yelled to notify one another, we gently picked them up behind their front legs and heeding Mom's warning, carried them at-arms length for their trip to the front porch. A red metal five-gallon can was their new temporary home and Dad supervised every capture to make sure that each toad was laid gently on the bottom of the can.

Though the toads must have been frustrated, none were ever hurt. After a half an hour or so, my father would call an end to the hunt, and send us in to take baths and get ready for bed. It was a successful hunt if we caught a half dozen of the unwilling participants. After we were inside, Dad released them back into the yard, and we no doubt caught the same toads many times over the summer.

By the time the evening toad hunt was concluded, Mom would have finished washing the dishes and prepared my bath. Our home had no running water or indoor plumbing, which was not uncommon for families like ours. Mom heated water in a bucket on a kerosene kitchen stove, then poured it into a number three galvanized wash tub in the middle of the kitchen. When the temperature of the water was deemed to be satisfactory, I washed under Mom's supervision being careful to wash thoroughly in order to meet her exacting standards. Once clean, dried, and dressed in pajamas, I was hugged and sent to the double bed that I shared with my brother. Leon soon followed and we would discuss the hunt and argue about who caught the most toads, who caught the biggest one and discuss why Mom did not like to hunt toads.

Once we were in bed, our parents would take their baths in the dark, by the outdoor hand pump, not twenty feet from our bedroom window. We could hear these young lovers giggling as they soaped each other up, no doubt hugging, touching, caressing and kissing. The giggling stopped abruptly when they finally rinsed themselves with a bucket of cold pump water. Leon and I were too young to understand, but enjoyed listening to them before we drifted off to sleep. They were our parents and we loved them,

Our family was content with the rhythms of our small town rural life but that was all changed when the Japanese bombed Pearl Harbor on December 7, 1941. Although he was not drafted until October, 1944, Dad eventually served in the Army's battle for Luzon in the Philippines Campaign. It was a defining period in his life.

CHAPTER FOUR

PREPARING FOR WAR

Although Dad was not called until the war was nearly three years old, my parents knew that ultimately he would be drafted. Rationing was nationwide and victory gardens were expected of everyone. Gasoline, rubber tires, sugar, and lard were just some of the everyday necessities that were in short supply. Black-out drills were common. Young men with no wife or children had been called first by our local draft board. Those with families, especially those with young children, served later in the conflict.

Communities collected scrap metal to meet the metal demands of war. Both ends of tin cans were cut out and the cans mashed flat for recycling. Mom gave me the job of flattening tin cans with a hammer. She could have done it quicker but it made me feel that I was helping in a significant way. The tin foil on gum wrappers and food packages was saved, rolled into a ball and taken to school by my brother, Leon, to show support for the troops. It was total war and everyone was expected to do their part.

When flattening the tin cans, I began to repetitively repeat something that I had heard from Uncle Leon. Every time I hit a can I would say "God damn Japs." My brother Leon egged me on, knowing that Mom would someday hear me, and I would be in trouble. When she finally heard me, I got a switching with a branch from the Camphor tree, and a lecture on using better language.

In an effort to prepare our family for the time when he

would not be there, Dad saved money, paid off the debt on their car and tried to start a supplemental income business for my mother. On a trip to Rolls Grocery Store, he had observed that with meat being in short supply that the price for rabbits was high. And so a plan was laid to start a small commercial rabbit business.

In short order, and with Uncle Leon's help, Dad constructed eight rabbit hutches that were four feet square and stood four feet off the ground on wooden posts. The hutches had wooden roofs and mesh wire for the sides and floor. Each hutch contained a birthing box filled with hay to protect the newborns.

With housing in hand, all they needed was seven does and a buck which Dad located in Orlando. Some of the does were brown and others were white. The buck was a very large brown bunny with big floppy ears. It was somewhat aggressive when handled. Leon was given the responsibility of feeding and watering them and I tagged along hoping to catch a glimpse of baby rabbits. The does would sometimes let you pet them.

Soon we had our first furry little rabbits and I was allowed to hold them. In no time we had lots of baby rabbits. And then we were overwhelmed with baby rabbits! Rabbits grow fast and soon the hutches were crowded with market sized young animals. The feed bill was getting larger as well. An ad was placed in the paper "Rabbits for sale. Live or dressed." Only two people came that week; both wanted pets.

The ad ran for two more weeks but there were no sales of dressed or live rabbits. My father dressed one of the young bucks but Mom said that she could not eat it after it had been a pet, even though wild cottontail rabbits had been regular supper fare for our family. Faced with the probability that things would not change, Dad and Uncle Leon killed and dressed all of the rabbits and wholesaled them in Orlando. My mother cried that weekend.

Dad had always hunted wild cottontails. They were

plentiful in the pastureland surrounding our home hiding under blackberry briars and palmettos. Dad used a single shot 22 caliber rifle and stalked his quarry to get a clean head shot. Mom fried them in a large iron skillet. Now that there would be no domestic rabbits to supplement the family's budget or the larder, he decided to teach Leon to hunt with the riffle. Although very young, Leon proved to be a good hunter and provided us with a great many suppers while Dad was away.

Mom was an accomplished fisherman and it was she who taught me to love fishing. Our family often fished on weekends. We used cane poles with worms dug from almost any rich or mucky soil. Worms were excellent bait for a wide variety of bream and catfish. Rarely did we catch a bass. We fished small creeks, ponds, and lake shorelines and we kept almost anything that we caught. Leon would scale the bream and an adult would do the knife work. Catfish had to be skinned which required more strength than Leon had, so Dad took care of that effort. Later when Dad was away Leon grew stronger and took over that responsibility as well.

Knowing that rental property is subject to the whims of landlords, Mom and Dad bought their first home on October 18, 1944. It was a large white frame home on Limit Street, now named Thacker Avenue. The house had electricity, indoor plumbing and running water. In the back there was room for a very large garden. A stand-alone building with a dirt floor served as storage and garage. The house had large front and back porches. A small grove of guavas grew on the west side of the house. They had chosen their first home well.

Mom was happy that that there was a family across the street who had a boy about my age, giving me someone to play with. We spent time at both houses and in the barn on their property. Like other old barns it was filled with objects that fascinate young boys. Boxes full of rusty relics were in the attic, and after Dad was away, we once found a round cardboard container with about a hundred pennies in it. The pennies were different than the ones that we usually bummed off our parents. Instead of Lincoln, they had pictures of Indians on the coins. It had been someone's coin collection. Unencumbered by honesty, and knowing nothing of their value, we were excited to find this cache because we now had money for penny candy. We took several coins down to the store that sold candy and thought ourselves rich. The boy across the street later spent the entire coin collection on penny treats.

When Dad finally left to go to the war, he arranged to have his fifty dollar monthly Army stipend sent directly to Mom, a practice common among GI's heading for the great conflict. He now realized that Mom would be able to take care of our family. She was a strong young women who had been challenged her whole life. His future was not so certain

Dad was sent to Camp Blanding for basic training. When his training was complete, he had a weekend pass and sent for Mom, Leon and I to join him. Once he left for basic training, Mom had taken a job in the Post Exchange at the Army Air Base. When Leon got home from school on that Friday, she loaded up our Ford sedan and headed for Green Cove Springs, which is just east of Camp Blanding. Soon it was dark, and Mom was unfamiliar with the roads. She was worried, but continued on through the darkness. She had not seen Dad for several weeks and we were all anxious to be with him. Finally, the city limit sign of Green Cove Springs came into view and Mom relaxed.

My father had rented a room with two double beds at a motel in the middle of that small town. Most of the rooms were filled with GIs with passes and their wives or girlfriends. Everywhere there was excitement and laughter. After Mom and Dad embraced and unloaded our possessions, off we went to find something to eat. The town was full of soldiers on leave so Dad took us to the only place that had seating. It was a soda fountain and all of the tables were full so we sat on stools at the counter.

A young waitress behind the counter began to notice the white haired, snaggeled-toothed five-year old and Dad put me up to asking her "What's cookin, good lookin?" With a big smile she fired back "Chicken, you wanna neck?" My parents and a few of the soldiers got a big laugh. I enjoyed the attention.

For two nights the young lovers were reunited. On Sunday, Dad returned to the base and we headed back to Kissimmee, this time in daylight. Mom was happy and so were Leon and I.

A short time later, Dad returned home for a short visit, then boarded the train in Kissimmee on his journey to the war in the Pacific. We would not see him again until February 1946.

CHAPTER FIVE

THE HOME FRONT IN A TIME OF WAR

With Dad away, Uncle Leon checked on our family every few days. He lived about a quarter mile away in a house he rented from two unmarried sisters that resided in Huntington, West Virginia. The two women came once each year and stayed for a few weeks to escape the cold. The house had once been a good home but the sisters would not replace the rusted tin roof and it leaked when it rained. Buckets were strategically placed on the floor to catch the drips. Parts of the ceiling plaster had fallen. Uncle Leon was a bachelor and the disrepair did not seem to bother him enough to replace the badly rusted tin roof himself, but periodically he did repair the leaks with tar.

There was no water on the premises and he hauled drinking water in three five-gallon and five one-gallon glass jugs from an artesian well. The well was located at the slaughterhouse where he butchered cattle every Thursday. Water for bathing, washing dishes and watering his horse was captured from the roof gutters and saved in steel barrels. The barrels were covered with a flat piece of tin and held in place with a brick, to keep out debris and insects. Several wells had been drilled on the property but the fine-grained Florida sand always clogged the point on the well, and made it impossible to continue drawing water. After several attempts, he had given up trying to get a productive well.

The fine sand and no water made it impossible to have grass in the yard but there were guava trees, a Suriname cherry, two century plants, a night blooming jasmine bush and a large camphor tree. A chinaberry tree shaded the outhouse which stood about one hundred feet behind the house.

Uncle Leon had lived in the house for many years and had never married. It was clearly a bachelor's home with a few essential pieces of furniture. An ancient leather couch, a hand cranked Victrola, two wooden chairs and a table with a large collection of country music records were in the living room. Roy Acuff's "Great Speckled Bird" and Earnest Tubb's "I am Walking The Floor Over You," were among his favorites.

Another table with six chairs and a stand-alone cabinet for storing canned goods were in the dining room. The kitchen contained a kerosene stove and a table for everyday meals. In the kitchen there was an ice-box, but it had not been used since his mother died. There were two bedrooms. Each one had a double bed, one small table with a kerosene lamp, a trunk to hold blankets, and a closet to hang clothes.

Off the kitchen and adjacent to the back door was a room used to store feed, hay, tools, rolls of barbed wire and other ranch supplies. A smaller room was entered from the dining room and was used to store saddles and other tack needed to ride horses. The saddle room also contained a cot for an occasional overnight guest, and a very old and rare double-barreled, ten gauge shotgun that his father had left him. It had not been fired for a long time, but he kept it and said that it was the only thing that he inherited from "the old man."

Our family often went to Uncle Leon's house for Sunday dinner. He and Dad were close. They would talk about the war and other things and he enjoyed having Mom cook a meal for him. He raised a lot of free-range chickens and sold the eggs to the local grocery stores. Many of the eggs and often a chicken were given to families who were on hard times. When we came for Sunday dinner, he would catch a pullet, then skin and clean it for Mom to cook. He never plucked them like most people did.

Mom served up three different menus for Sunday dinner: fried chicken, chicken and dumplings or chicken and rice. Cooked vegetables and dessert varied based upon their availability. All of her Sunday meals were greatly enjoyed and everyone looked forward to being together for a mid-day feast. My brother and I always got a leg even when we protested.

When we left to go home, Uncle Leon always gave us a paper bag with a week's supply of eggs. If we needed more eggs later in the week Mom dispatched Leon or me to his house to fetch another dozen or so. His house was never locked, and we were free to enter once we convinced his working dogs to let us pass. During Dads time away, Mom sometimes needed a few canned goods to carry her through the week. She would write a note and send us to Uncle Leon's to pick out what we needed. We continued to observe our Sunday dinner routine while Dad was away; it helped make everyone feel normal.

Only once did we ever pluck any of the birds. Uncle Leon had an order for a few dozen dressed chickens while Dad was gone. Mom heated water in her cast iron wash pot with a fire made from fatty pine roots called "lighter'd knots." She then dipped the chickens into the hot water after Uncle Leon had caught the chickens and chopped off their heads, using a hatchet and a chopping block. My brother and I were charged with removing the feathers. Dipping the birds in hot water makes it possible to more easily pull out their feathers. It was a time consuming and unpleasant process. Mom would inspect each bird when we finished and make sure that they were free of pin feathers. Uncle Leon then finished dressing the birds and delivered them to market.

My brother Leon now stepped up and began hunting rabbits. After school and on the weekends, he stalked the pastures near our home to help Mom provide for us. Mom worried about a nine-year old with a rifle but realized that Dad had taught him well, and there were never any unintended consequences.

On Thursdays, Uncle Leon would stop by with meat scraps left from butchering the four head of beef cattle for which he had a standing order. He also brought cattle brains and sometimes tripe because they had little market value. The brains were cleaned, separated into smaller pieces and sautéed with scrambled eggs. Leon and I hated them. Nevertheless, Mom cooked them and seemed to enjoy her meal.

Preparing beef tripe was a bigger chore. Tripe consists of the four stomachs that cattle have to digest the grass that they eat. After the grass is ingested it ferments in each of the four stomachs. Cattle will belch up the fermenting grass and chew it again to speed up digestion, hence the phrase "chewing the cud". Preparing tripe for eating starts with careful washing of the stomach to thoroughly clean it. Then it is cut into serving size pieces and boiled to tenderize it. It may be eaten boiled but was more often fried after it had been boiled. It tasted better than it sounds.

Syrup was a special treat and one day Uncle Leon picked us up and took us to a farm off the Vineland Road. The farmer grew sugarcane and there were several families gathered to harvest it and make syrup. A mule was harnessed to a long pole that provided power to the mill. As the mule walked endlessly in a circle, cane stalks were fed between the mill stones at the center of the machine. Cane juice flowed into a large metal bucket prior to being transported to a large wood-fired cast-iron pot, where it was boiled down to make syrup. Periodically someone would collect some of the juice and share it around. It was sweet, and a break in the labor was appreciated. At the end of the day, every family received a container of syrup to take home. Syrup making was as much a social event as a necessity.

Other people also helped our family. Knowing that Dad was at war, a Chinese truck farmer we called Grandpa Lee would give me a Chinese cabbage when I was over playing with his grandson, Charley. "For your Mama," he would say and then smile. I never knew him by any other name. He was the patriarch of the Lee family. His two sons Tommy and Lawrence ran the field operations and Grandpa Lee oversaw the packing house. Approaching one hundred years in age he was still active. On Saturday afternoons he would attend the local theater to see western movies along with his grandchildren and at least two hundred other kids. He was probably the only adult in the theater. If you were around when his daughter-in-law loaded him into the station wagon he would often take you as well. Once there, he paid the nine-cent admission and bought each one of us a ten-cent box of popcorn. He was a very kind man and much admired by everyone who knew him.

Throughout this period Mom was resourceful and we never missed a meal. She took us fishing when she could, and my brother cleaned what we caught. We ate the rabbits that Leon brought home, and the food supplied by Uncle Leon and our neighbor Grandpa Lee.

Uncle Leon would continue to look after us until Dad returned. He was a good and decent man with a big heart and a soft spot for those who needed help.

CHAPTER SIX

AFTER THE WAR

Following the disaster on the night when he first returned no one knew what to expect from my father. He seemed normal as he settled in to his new life. It was as if nothing had ever happened. He returned to being an electrician, this time starting his own business. With the baby boom in full swing, business was good and he hired a young assistant to help with the work. I never knew the assistant's full name. Everyone called him "Little Joe." On Saturdays and in the summer, they took my brother Leon on jobs to be an extra set of hands.

In 1946, while we were living on Limit Street, Dad surprised Leon and me with the purchase of two calves and told us that they were ours to care for. We promptly named them and fed them a powdered milk supplement using a bucket with a rubber nipple. I named mine Pepsi Cola Pete and thought that I had a pet for life. When Pete would suck he would get excited and butt the bucket. The first time that he did that I dropped the bucket and spilled the milk. Dad was not happy and threatened to give Pete to Leon. I never dropped it again. Leon named his calf but he was not confused about their ultimate destiny. Several months later when the calves had grown larger, Dad sold them without telling us, and used the money to buy Leon a horse. I, on the other hand, was caught unaware and upset at the loss of my calf.

The mare was named Pal. Leon had wanted a horse for a long time and he was ecstatic. Dad and Uncle Leon had chosen the horse from a local ranch and hauled it home. Pal was to be kept at Uncle Leon's house with his horse, Fanny, because we had no fenced enclosure for the horse. Leon started riding with Uncle Leon every Sunday afternoon when he checked his cattle. Between rides he would go over to curry the animal. My brother and Uncle Leon were forming a close bond on their Sunday rides.

Mom and Dad started inviting friends over for weekend dinners and parties, and in turn our family was invited to share reciprocal hospitality. On such occasions there were kids playing, adults laughing and stories shared of fun times from their past. Food was plentiful and so was whiskey. During Saturday night parties the drinking often lasted far into the night. It was in the first few months following his return that dad began to show signs of a serious drinking problem. At first the whiskey made him happy and often the life of the party. Later in the evening, after the evening meal was finished, and the women had washed the dishes, Dad and the other men continued smoking cigarettes and drinking at an accelerated pace. He was soon over the edge, and the talk would turn serious. The stories now were about the war.

There were two stories that he could never reconcile. He had survivor's guilt. The first involved the death of a friend. Dad and his friend were pinned down in a fox hole and under heavy fire from superior Japanese forces. The enemy was firing small arms at will and were using mortars to great advantage against the American forces. As the mortars crept ever closer, a retreat was ordered. Dad and his friend debated who would offer covering fire and who would retreat first. They decided that his friend would go first. When his friend left their fox hole he was gunned down by a volley of machine gun fire not ten feet from their place of cover. Dad watched him twitch, moan and die. Somehow, Dad escaped when he retreated but he never forgot the terror of that moment, nor the loss of his friend.

The second story also involved a retreat. Japanese forces

were again advancing, and he could see that to maintain contact with his unit he needed to traverse a narrow mountain trail. The trail made a sharp turn after being exposed for about fifty feet on a ledge along the cliff face. He made his way along the path but when he turned the corner, he encountered a young Japanese soldier coming from the other direction. Both were so surprised that they withdrew without firing their weapons. Now Dad and the young Japanese soldier were faced with a dilemma. Both needed to advance to the corner of the cliff face, and the one to arrive second was going to be exposed and die. Drawing as much courage as he could, he charged to the corner, arrived first and shot the young soldier at close range. The image of that soldier's face as he fell mortally wounded off the cliff haunted him for the rest of his life.

When telling these stories Dad would weep and lament that they were just young men like himself. They would never have a chance for a full life and for one of them, he was responsible. All of the other fire fights did not seem to bother him as much.

Growing up, I heard these stories many times when Dad was drinking heavily. I never knew whether the memories brought on the heavy drinking or if the drinking was preamble to the memories.

Dad's drinking problem became more frequent, and occasionally he was violent. Mom took the brunt of it, but sometimes Leon and I did as well. He would return to the same tired accusations of infidelity that he made on his first night home. Their marriage was now in trouble. She had more than a few bruises and black eyes. When he beat her, she began leaving the house but never went far. She would let him cool off and go to bed. The next morning it would be as if nothing had happened the night before. She was trying to hold their marriage together at great cost to her personal safety. She always forgave him, but he never changed.

When he was not drinking heavily, life was good. We

planted a large garden, went fishing, and he threw a baseball to Leon and me. The Sunday dinners with Uncle Leon had stopped. Although a heavy drinker at an earlier age, Uncle Leon had quit drinking many years before after being diagnosed with diabetes. He did not approve of Dad's downward spiral and made little effort to conceal it. The weekly allotment of eggs was discontinued.

We kept visiting friends, aunts, uncles and cousins but the circle of those who could overlook Dad's behavior was shrinking. One couple who continued to be friends was Coy Yates and his wife, Belle. Coy was the overseer of a large ranch on Pleasant Hill Road. They lived in a nice frame house at the entrance to the property. We sometimes spent the weekend at their house, arriving on Friday evening and leaving on Sunday at noon. It was always a lot of fun.

On one particular visit Mom played a trick on Dad that had every one laughing. By Saturday afternoon the adults realized that the spirits were growing low and that a run for groceries was called for. Mom was elected to make the long trip back to town for supplies. Resigned to the realization that she had fought the good fight and lost, she took the car and left. On the way to town she saw a small alligator crossing the road. He was about two feet long. A strong cracker woman, Mom was no shrinking violet. She slammed on the brakes and gave chase to the startled animal, catching it just before it reached the safety of the road side ditch. My mother put the gator in the trunk of the car and continued on to town.

When her errands were finished, she loaded her stores into the back seat floorboard of the car and went back to the ranch. Normally she would have put the groceries in the trunk of the car. We children ran to meet her when she arrived at the house knowing that she would bring us candy. She greeted us with instructions to stand back, be quiet and watch. She then called to my father who now was feeling no pain "Rowdy, would you come here and carry these groceries into the house?" Rowdy was Dad's nickname, a title he had earned from bar confrontations in our small town. Dad staggered out and raised the trunk lid only to jump back after being startled by the gator in defensive position showing a sea of teeth. Everybody had a good laugh at his expense and after he recovered, he also thought that the prank had been well played. The gator was recaptured, and kept in the metal watering trough beneath the wind mill until he again was transported in the trunk of our car, back to town. Spending the night in our bath tub, he at last was taken to the zoo and released into a new home. I watched him grow up over the next several years as I also grew to be an awkward teenager

Dad's drinking was getting worse and he now had trouble finding electrical work. He was often sullen but at other times he was pleasant and outgoing. He started hanging out at bars and he sometimes brought Leon and me with him. Intending to stop for only one drink, he would leave us in the car, while he went inside. Once inside he would lose track of time and we waited for an hour or more. Mom was never pleased once we returned home to a meal that had grown cold.

In order to pick up the missing income from his failing electrical business, Dad and Little Joe went into a side business. Dad bought and modified a pickup truck to haul fish from the coast which were then sold to people in the town's neighborhoods. My grandfather, Will, lived in Titusville and had built a smoker using corrugated tin roofing sheets and metal racks. He dry-smoked mullet using green bay magnolia wood and sold it locally to stores and bars, and to a steady stream of people who wanted the smoked delicacies. Dad started sending Little Joe over to Titusville on Thursdays to buy smoked mullet from Grandpa Will which they then put in cellophane bags and sold as counter food to local bars in Kissimmee for thirty five cents each. On Friday morning fresh mullet also were purchased from a commercial fish house, then packed in ice for the journey home.

Early Saturday morning, Little Joe and I would head out to sell fresh mullet to the people of Kissimmee. Little Joe drove the truck down each street of our small town. He weighed out each purchase, wrapped the fish in newspaper and collected the money. I ran from house to house, knocked on the door and asked "Do you want to buy some fresh mullet for supper? Ten cents a pound, three pounds for a quarter." Most people immediately said no, but we quickly learned that if someone said yes, those who had just refused often came out of their homes, looked over our fish and would buy some. Little Joe always took his time weighing and wrapping the fish, all the while engaging the customer in small talk. It was good for business.

Over time the fish business was seen to be unprofitable and Dad's electrical business also was not prospering. We had all grown fond of Little Joe but the time had come when Dad could no longer afford to keep him. Joe often ate with us and sometimes slept at our house. He had no family that we knew of and when he left I never saw him again.

Even though their marriage was falling apart. Mom became pregnant and my sister Denise was born in 1947. Both parents were thrilled to have a little girl now that Leon and I were growing older. We all doted on her and for a time there was less tension in our house. The magic did not last.

Dad was away at bars a lot now and Mom was growing tired of his absence. When he came home late at night they argued. Once in 1948, when he came home drunk and began to be physical, she disappeared out the back door. Enraged by her absence, Dad told me to get into the back seat of the car. He had bought a second hand car with a spot light mounted on the drivers-side door. When he came out to the car, he had his old 22-caliber rifle with him and a box of bullets. For the next twenty minutes he drove up and down the dirt roads near our home shining the spot light and shooting at anything that moved. I was terrified.

Mom did not come home that night, preferring to go to a friend's house. Shortly thereafter, Mom, Leon, Denise and I moved back to the house by the railroad, where we had lived before Dad went to war. They were now legally separated, and their divorce was imminent. The house on Limit Street was sold on October 27, 1948. With their divorce finalized in early 1949, Dad wasted no time marrying Iona May Ivey on March 1, 1949. My mother took her three kids and moved to a rental house on Old Dixie Highway. It was the road to the Stockyards.

CHAPTER SEVEN

STOCKYARD ROAD - THE OLD DIXIE HIGHWAY

The house on the road to the stockyards was a major step down in living, but it was all that Mom could afford. Where she found the money to keep us going was a mystery because she did not have a job when we first moved there.

The house was a small unpainted frame building composed of four equal sized rooms. Two of them were bedrooms, another room served as a living room while the fourth room was a combination kitchen and eating area. There was no indoor plumbing or running water in the house. Water was taken from an outdoor hand pump near the back door. An outhouse was at the back of the property. A fireplace provided the only heat source. We seldom had wood to burn, so it was basically useless. Each room had an electric wall switch to operate the single light bulb hanging from the ceiling and there was a single electric outlet in three of the rooms. The kitchen had two additional outlets. Mom cooked on a kerosene stove and we ate on a small table that was provided by the landlord. She washed our clothes with a rub board and a galvanized wash tub that sat on a small bench by the hand pump.

Previous occupants had nailed cardboard to the studs that separated the rooms to provide privacy and a cloth hung in the door way to each of the bedrooms. The walls were not insulated and the boards that composed the outer walls were not tightly fitted. On winter days when the wind blew, the house was cold and drafty.

There were four frame houses by the road. We had the smallest building, the only one with no front or back porch. The other houses were larger, had porches in front and back, and were in much better condition than ours. A sawmill was located across the road, and all of the outer walls of the houses looked like they had been built with the rough sawed lumber that was their specialty. The owners of the sawmill may well have been the land lords.

Uncle Leon again began checking on us now and then as he hauled cattle to the stockyards on Wednesdays, or when he picked up the cattle that he was commissioned to slaughter on Thursdays. He resumed a regular delivery of eggs, beef scraps and live chickens. Dad was nowhere to be seen, but perhaps he was helping financially.

At first, my brother Leon and I shared a double bed in the front bedroom and Mom and Denise shared the other bedroom. That soon changed.

Mom was now struggling to take care of us. Less than a month after we moved into the new house it was decided that Leon would go and live with Uncle Leon. He was eleven years old and thrilled with the move. I watched him drive off with Uncle Leon in the old 1939 Ford cattle truck without ever looking back. My brother had been a stabilizing force in my life and now he was gone. I missed him before the truck was out of sight.

With Leon gone, I got to know the McDaniel family next door. They had the biggest house among the four and a family large enough to need one. There were several children in the McDaniel family and they were as poor as we were. The range of children's ages was more than fifteen years and they all pitched in to help with family chores. Everyone had been taught to spring into action to help the youngest child, Andy, who suffered from serious and frequent epileptic seizures. At the first sign of trouble some would hold him down while others placed a spoon into his mouth to keep him from biting his tongue. The whole episode was disturbing to watch.

Their son L.V. was a year older than me but was in my grade in school. He became my friend and we spent a lot of time together. I soon learned that L.V. had a unique physical feature that surely was a sign from God that he was one of the chosen ones. L.V. had eleven toes and I was amazed. On his right foot he had two little toes, one above the other. To accommodate this problem he had cut a hole in his shoe and the extra toe peaked out above the leather. At school some of the other boys liked to "accidentally" step on the toe and a dust-up often ensued. He was a tough boy and always prevailed in those situations. He and I never argued and got along well.

One day, after I had been living at the house on the road to the stockyards for a few months, L.V. motioned to me to follow him in to a small patch of guava trees about fifty paces behind our two houses. When we arrived at our destination, he proudly produced the secret that he was about to share. His mother Mrs. Ada McDaniel dipped snuff almost continually. She bought it in sufficient quantities to ensure that she was never out of the one simple vice that she allowed herself. L.V. had snitched a small can from her cache of Sweet Peach Snuff and we were about to try it for the first time. We had watched her pull out her lower lip and pour in the snuff and were sure that there was nothing more to it. Being in possession of the contraband, L.V. chose to go first. Pulling out his lower lip he began pouring in a generous portion. Unfortunately, neither of us had ever observed that his mother Ada held her breath when filling her lip. Unfortunately, L.V. took a deep breath, filling his lungs with the brown powdered tobacco and immediately fell to the ground on his hands and knees. There he writhed and coughed in obvious distress for a few seconds until I ran to his house yelling, "Come quick Mrs. McDaniel. I think L.V. is dying." When she got to the guava patch L.V. was sitting up but still coughing up thick brown mucus. He continued to do so for the rest of the day. We both got a stern lecture but no punishment. I think that our mothers thought that L.V. had suffered enough and that we had learned an important lesson. I never again wanted to try snuff.

The McDaniel family turned out to be true friends. When Mom and Dad had separated in 1948, Mom was in the early stages of pregnancy. By the time that first winter arrived she was probably seven months into her term and visibly showing. A cold spell had moved down to central Florida and we had experienced a very cold night in the poorly built and unheated house. Cold wind had blown through the cracks and the quilts had not been enough.

Early that morning I heard my mother call out to me to hurry into her room. When I did I was shocked at what I saw. She had thrown off the quilts that she and Denise had slept under and the sheets were soaked in blood. She told me to go next door and fetch Mrs. McDaniel. I ran barefoot next door and explained the situation. She and her oldest daughter followed me home and after surveying the situation sent me with my sister, Denise, to her house to have breakfast. They were now in charge.

Breakfast at the McDaniel's house was different than anything that I had ever experienced. Everyone ate at a long hand-made table with attached benches, like those seen at public parks. Mrs. McDaniel had made a huge batch of biscuits and everyone had biscuits with apple butter or cane syrup and strong coffee. This was the breakfast for adults, teens and preteens. Toddlers and infants drank watered down canned milk. I had never been allowed to have coffee before and drank a large cup. I ate my fill of biscuits and apple butter and waited to be called home. Ada's daughter brought some fresh milk from our icebox for Denise to drink.

Later that morning Ada's daughter came for me and said to bring a shovel from their tool bin. She was about twenty years old and was small for her age. I later learned that she had been a premature baby and her mother said that she had been so small at birth, that her first crib was a shoe box. Born at home, they did not expect her to live.

Upon returning to our house Mrs. McDaniel took me outside and pointed to a place by the chimney and told me to dig a hole. She then went back inside to attend my mother. I was still barefoot, having failed to put on shoes before going to get help for Mom. The cold metal of the shovel stung my feet and after a while I went inside to report my progress. Mrs. McDaniel came out, looked at the hole and said that it was not nearly deep enough. With hand motions she showed me the dimensions that she wanted and once again went inside.

I continued digging until the hole was big enough. I called into the back door and Mrs. McDaniel and her daughter came outside. Mrs. McDaniel was carrying the bloody sheets. Approaching the hole that I had dug, she handed the bundle to me and instructed me to lay it gently on the bottom. By the weight of the bundle I knew that it was the fetus that Mom had been carrying, and that the hole I had dug was now a grave. She then told me to fill the hole and to dig up a small hibiscus-like plant called Turk's Cap and plant it at the top when I finished. It was the only flowering plant in that God-forsaken yard. I did so under her silent supervision. No one ever mentioned that morning again.

Mrs. McDaniel checked in on my mother twice daily and brought our family food until my mother fully recovered. Her kindness was appreciated and has never been forgotten.

The events of that day remain fresh in my memory after all these years. I was only nine years old at the time, but now realize that I did a lot of growing up on that one cold morning.

CHAPTER EIGHT

GEIGER'S FISH CAMP

In the summer of 1949, I went to live with Dad. Mom had recovered her health but was struggling financially to care for Denise and me. Dad had remarried and Mom felt that he and his new bride, Iona, could help by taking me for the summer. I was somewhat unsure about living with him but had no other choice. A few phone calls were exchanged, and the deal was sealed.

Two days after the school year ended, Dad arrived driving the skeeter that was his only source of transportation. Dad's skeeter was a modified Model A Ford that had most of the body removed. From the dashboard and steering wheel forward, the auto was intact but the side panels to the engine compartment had been removed to help keep the engine cool. The front seat and remainder of the cabin had been replaced with a wooden seat and a wooden bed, effectively making it an open-air pickup truck. To start the engine Dad used a hand crank and I soon learned that he often cussed the vehicle when it was hard to start or when he skinned his knuckles while spinning the motor.

After brief goodbyes, Dad and I left for an eight-week stay at his house by the Saint John's River. When we arrived, I was surprised to find that it wasn't a house at all. It was a wooden house boat! And it was not in the water. The boat had been stranded following a flood of the St. John's River the year before, and was now high and dry until the next flood. It sat upright, held in place by strategically placed timbers. Steps had been built to permit easy access to the rear of the boat. It sat no more than one hundred feet from the river and instantly stirred the imagination of a ten-year-old boy. It was the start of a good summer.

Iona greeted me warmly. I had not yet met her and I was apprehensive that she might not want me around. She quickly put my fears to rest with a hug and a glass of ice-cold sweet tea. It did not take long until I felt perfectly at ease in my new surroundings. The boat had a galley, a sitting area, a double bed for Dad and Iona and a bunk bed for me. There was no electricity in the boat, so kerosene lamps were used for lighting. Although there was a head (bathroom) on the boat it could not be used while on land. I quickly learned that I could pee where ever I liked, but the other daily need required Dad or me to take a shovel plus a roll of toilet paper and walk a trail into the Spartina dominated landscape. Switch grass was what we called Spartina in the fifties. We had never heard the word Spartina.

Uncomfortable at first, I soon learned to adjust to the new expectations. For modesty, Iona used a chamber pot which was kept in the head and emptied daily in the Spartina using the same shovel that Dad and I used.

The boat resided at Geiger's Fish Camp on the southwest corner of the intersection of highway 46 and the St. Johns River. In the summer of 1949, the fish camp consisted of a small frame building on stilts high enough to keep if above water when the river flooded. The owners, an older couple, welcomed me to my new home. Their business consisted of renting a few boats with motors, and selling bait, tackle, soft drinks, beer, peanuts and other snacks. They had electricity and used a refrigerator to cool soft drinks and beer. Customers parked on the shoulder of the highway and crossed a narrow wooden catwalk to the building that served as the Geiger home and place of business. Steep wooden steps led down from their porch to the ground and provided access to the river where the boats were kept and to our landlocked houseboat. Water for cooking and drinking was collected from the roof of the Geiger's home in metal barrels that were covered with white muslin cloth to keep mosquitoes from laying eggs. It became my job to fetch drinking water using a white enamel bucket, thereby saving Iona the trip up the long flight of stairs, and to bring water from the river which was boiled before washing dishes.

When the evening meal was served on the day I arrived, I ate spaghetti with meat balls for the first time. She had made it especially for me. After dinner it was time for a bath and, for the second time that day, I learned that life on a house boat was different. We took our baths in the river wearing bathing suits. Iona had bought one for me in preparation for my visit. The dark water was stained with tannin and there was a thin layer of mud on the bottom of the river. I was taught to do the stingray shuffle to reduce the chance that I would step on a ray and be injured by its barbed tail. Bathing now took some getting used to, nevertheless I was getting adjusted to a new routine and I liked most of it.

Earlier in the spring, Dad had embarked on a new way to make a living. He sometimes still worked as an electrician but in the new community there was not enough steady work to meet his family's needs. He was trapping catfish out of Lake Harney. In the cooler months he had been successful with traps made of chicken wire. The traps were round with two cone openings one foot apart in one end, and a trap release at the other. The first cone was pointed downward and the second was pointed in the opposite direction making it difficult for the fish to find their way out of the trap once they entered. Each of his thirty traps was baited with pieces of hard-pressed grain cakes that were held together with rubber bands cut from old tire inner tubes. Each bait consisted of six by twelve inch pieces of soybean, cottonseed and peanut cake. The bait held up well in the water and catfish were attracted to it. All of the commercial fishermen used the same combination for bait.

When summer came, the lake had warmed and traps no longer were effective. A heavy coating of algae had attached to the wire and fish avoided the entrance. Dad and the other fishermen had pulled their traps and let them dry in the sun. He now spent a lot of time with a wire brush to get rid of the heavy coat of dead algae attached to the wire. It was hard, sweaty, nasty work but he never complained. When there was other work available, he took it, but it was never enough to meet our family's needs.

Dad and Iona were happy that first summer they were married. His dark moods were now nearly gone, and he rarely drank to excess. The stories of war seldom were told and he laughed a lot. I don't remember a single time when he was harsh with her or me. The skeeter was not so fortunate because it often would not start.

There were cane poles rigged for fishing at the houseboat, and lots of free time for a boy now ten years old. Worms were easily dug for bait from the soft soil in the river bank, and fish were plentiful. I caught so many that I fed ourselves and the Giegers at least three times a week but most of the fish that I caught were tossed back after being carefully examined. I once caught an eel and thought that it was a snake. I had never seen an eel and I ran back to the house boat calling out "I caught a snake. I caught a snake." Dad came running over and had a good laugh when he saw what I had on my line. It was the only eel that I caught that summer.

Dad did not take me with him when he left to go to work like he had when Leon was young. I stayed at the fish camp and amused myself. Once each week, he and Iona drove to Sanford to buy groceries, beer, gas and various supplies. I was not invited, so I stayed home and fished while they had their day out. While in town, Iona took our clothes to a laundromat because she had no other means by which to wash them in clean water. There was not enough water in the barrels for washing clothes.

With Labor Day just around the corner, I was on the move again. Dad took me back to Kissimmee for the start of the school year. Mom had taken a job at Micklers Crate Mill and moved into a much nicer house in town. I was glad to be back with her and Denise. It had been a good summer.

CHAPTER NINE

DISASTER ON LAKE HARNEY

In 1949 the world was changing. In Europe, the Berlin Airlift ended on May 12th. The Soviet Union had tried to put a stranglehold on Berlin on June 24, 1948, by denying access to the Allies who controlled most of the city. Working with the East Germans who controlled the road to Berlin, the Soviets denied passage for almost a year. The Allies responded with a massive airlift to resupply the city and the Soviets and East Germans finally relented.

In Asia, the Communist leader, Mao Zedong, established The Republic of China, after defeating Chiang Kai-shek for control of the mainland. Chiang Kai-sheck and his Nationalist government were forced to retreat to the island of Taiwan.

And in Kissimmee Florida, I was dreading the fast approaching school year.

That September, I began the fifth grade under the veteran tutelage of Mrs. Murphy, the most dreaded teacher in the school system. She had a reputation for being a strict, no-nonsense disciplinarian who gave her students homework every night. This led to conflict because I considered homework to be optional. She, of course, quickly won that battle, and I soon concluded that memorizing multiplication tables, learning where countries were on a map and competing in spelling bees was the duty of every responsible citizen, especially skinny, white-haired boys!

At lunch time she sat at a table near the opening in the wall where soiled plates were scraped and passed through to a long, metal counter, prior to being washed. As part of her reign of terror, she required everyone to show her their dish before they handed them over to the person scraping plates. This caused more conflict. If there was any food left on your plate she made you sit next to her until all of your food was eaten. Every kid has some food that they despise. Mine was pickled beets. Fortunately, my friend, Ken Tufts, liked pickled beets but disliked sausage. That year we both learned the high art of bartering.

Although we were living in a better house and neighborhood Mom was still struggling to make ends meet. She worked at the crate mill to afford the house that she rented. We now lived in a painted house with electricity, indoor plumbing, running water, a phone and heat. It had a nice yard with big oaks between the sidewalk and the street. The house was situated about three blocks from the railroad track on East Vine Street. The location was convenient for me to walk to school and for Mom to walk to work or shop. A small grocery store run by German immigrants was just down the street, and a neighbor two doors down took care of Denise when Mom was at work. Things were looking up.

One Sunday morning, our doorbell rang and I answered it while Mom was preparing to cook our breakfast. There standing in front of me was a man in his early fifties, wearing soiled clothes, needing a haircut, and carrying a small cardboard suit case.

"Is your mother home?" he asked.

"Yes she is," I replied and called for her to come to the front door.

"Ma'am, pardon me for intruding, but I need something to eat. I am willing to work for my breakfast. I haven't eaten since noon yesterday," he said.

Mom looked him over, thought hard for a minute, and told him to go around the house and wait on the screened back porch, where there was a small table and two chairs. She told me to wait with him, and over the next half hour he told me that he was a hobo, and had just gotten off the train three blocks from our house. He had been traveling around the south, and was just passing through. I was mesmerized by the stories of the places that he had been. He had a gentle way of talking and when I brought out two additional chairs, Mom and Denise joined us at the little table with bacon, eggs, grits, coffee and milk. It was clear that he had not eaten in a while and I think that Mom had struggled enough in her life to want to share what we had to eat. After we finished our meal he asked if he could wash the dishes or rake the yard. He would do anything to repay Mom's kindness. Mom said no, and wished him good luck. I watched him as he walked back toward the railroad track and disappeared from view. Mom and I wondered where he would go next.

Mom was still a young woman needing a social life and she began dating again. She had several suitors that fall and winter but by the summer of 1950 had settled on a man named Billie Joe (last name withheld to protect his descendants privacy). Billie Joe lived in Orlando but his work frequently brought him to Kissimmee. He came to see her every Friday evening. Mom would prepare supper for Denise and me prior to going out for the night with Billie Joe to eat, drink, and be with friends. I would bathe and dress Denise for bed after they had gone, and later would turn-in when Denise fell asleep. Not long after Billie Joe began dating Mom, he began sleeping over and staying the weekend. He would return to Orlando after breakfast on Sunday. They slept late and I usually fed Denise her breakfast and ate some cereal before they arose.

It was obvious that Billie Joe enjoyed his time with my mother but it was equally obvious that he cared not for Denise and me. There was seldom a kind word from him for either of us, and he engineered the events of the weekend to see as little as possible of us. They frequently would go out on Saturday afternoon and leave me to care for Denise. I quickly learned to dislike him.

In February, 1951, I returned home from selling programs and soft drinks at the Silver Spurs Rodeo. I had worked at the annual summer rodeo event for a couple of years. It was a good way for a kid to earn a few bucks.

The Silver Spurs Rodeo was a major tourist attraction in Kissimmee. The first rodeo had been held on July 4, 1944, but now a February date had been added. By the eighties, this rapidly expanding event would grow into the biggest rodeo east of the Mississippi River with a purse of $60,000. It was designated the Official State Rodeo by the Florida Legislature in 1994.

I had thumbed a ride to the rodeo grounds and worked the parking lot, hawking programs for twenty five cents each. I got to keep a nickel on each sale. Most kids waited at the gates to approach customers, but I realized that there was an advantage to approaching the customers as soon as they got out of their cars. Once the rodeo started, I went in and sold soft drinks. In addition to the money, which was substantial for a kid my age, I got to see the rodeo.

One year Uncle Leon was recognized at the rodeo by the Florida Cattleman's Association, for his safe handling of cattle. I stood proudly as the citation was read over the PA system and he accepted his award.

After the rodeo was over, I bummed a ride home and handed the money over to Mom. She then said that she had something to tell me.

Mom knew that she was pregnant and she soon opened negotiations with Dad to take over the care of Denise and me. Although Dad had no phone, he had a friend with a phone who served as an intermediary. The calls went on for several days with Dad offering little sympathy or support. If he had been paying alimony, it surely had ended now. Phone conversations were bitter and often ended with Mom crying. Increasingly desperate, she gave Dad an ultimatum that he had to take

Denise and me until she gave birth and was back on her feet. She then prepared to leave. Mom did not want to deal directly with Dad. She asked the woman who watched Denise while I was in school if Denise and I could stay with her until Dad came to pick us up. The neighbor agreed to help as a go-between.

A few days later, Aunt Virginia stopped by to get Mom at mid-morning. Mom assured us that Dad would be there to pick us up in the afternoon. My mother then gave us a hug, loaded her few possessions in Virginia's car and left. I never knew what Mom's residence was during the next several months. Did she live with Billie Joe or with Virginia? We had no contact with her, and I never thought to ask. I assumed that she was with Billie Joe. Nevertheless, I never saw him again, nor did I care to.

Evening came and Dad had not come for us. Our host called and left several messages beginning about two in the afternoon. Dad did not respond. She fed us supper with her family, and we slept that night at her house. The next morning she again left Dad messages at intervals through-out the day. By mid-afternoon she began calling my mother, who in turn tried to contact Dad. She too was unsuccessful. By now our neighbor was growing a bit weary of the drama of which she was now a participant. There were muffled conversations between her and her husband and I was feeling a bit unsure of our situation. We slept over for a third night. On the fourth morning Dad called and capitulated saying that he would come get us. Our hosts were relieved to have us reunited with one of our parents, and with no further responsibility. They had treated us well, but I could feel the tension that Denise and I were causing. When Dad came he thanked her and made a few disparaging remarks about Mom, before the neighbor gave both of us a hug, and we left for Geneva, a small town on lake Harney that was to be our new home.

The ride to Geneva in the open skeeter was cold. It was

February and although the vehicle would not go faster than forty miles an hour, the wind cut through us. Neither of us were dressed warm enough so Denise, who was in the middle, sat as close to me as she could. Each of us held a large paper bag with the only clothes that we had. It helped buffer us from the wind. There was not much conversation. Dad was preoccupied with driving and the skeeter engine was noisy.

When we arrived in Geneva I was surprised that we did not go to the house boat at the river. He and Iona now rented an unpainted, frame house next to an orange grove. I would later learn that a barn in the grove housed a Model T Ford. The barn was unlocked and I could go in and sit in the automobile. I had never seen a Model T before.

The house had three bedrooms, a kitchen, a dining room and a living room. There was no electricity, running water, or indoor plumbing. A hand pump was accessible from the back porch making it unnecessary to walk into the sandy backyard to bathe or draw water for the house. An outhouse was located a short distance away, at the back of the property. We entered the house from the large front porch. On the right side of the porch stood one of three bedrooms.

Iona came out to greet us as soon as the engine was turned off. It was the first time that she and Denise had met. Although Iona was warm and friendly, Denise was tired and somewhat reserved. Over the last four days she had endured a great deal for a child not yet four years old.

My next surprise came moments later when a boy about the same age as Denise walked out the front door and down the steps. His name was Eddie and he was Iona's son by a previous marriage. Eddie had not been at the house boat when I visited in the summer of 1949. I never knew why, but now we were all one family. In time Denise would get to be more comfortable with her new living arrangements. She had never lived apart from her mother.

The final surprise came when I did not get one of the

bedrooms. Iona and Dad shared the largest bedroom. Eddie and Denise shared the smallest, and the third bedroom, which had a separate entrance off the front porch, was occupied by a man named Vernon. My cot had been set up in the living room which was seldom used for that purpose. I enjoyed the arrangement except when Dad and Vernon arose early to tend the fish traps.

Vernon stayed in his room until we were settled in. Fishing was good that year and Dad had brought him aboard to help with the work. They were fishing more traps now and Vernon was a good worker. A quiet man in his early sixties, he liked all three of us kids, and would spend time talking about anything we wanted to except his former life. I never knew his last name. He was not married and for a while I suppose that we were his family.

The following Monday, Iona took me down to the three-room school house in Geneva and enrolled me in school. I now had a beautiful young teacher who taught two grades in the same room.

About the second week we were with Dad and Iona, a major two-day winter storm hit central Florida. Dad and Vernon knew that the storm was coming after hearing about it on Dad's battery radio. Because batteries were expensive, Dad only listened to news on the radio once each day, mostly to find out how things were going in the Korean War under General MacArthur. The storm was the news on the previous night's broadcast.

Dad decided to run the traps before the storm arrived. The battery radio said that it would be a bad storm and that it might stick around for a while. They feared that there was not enough bait in the traps to keep fish alive for an extended period of time and that the cat fish might die before they could get back out on the lake. Arising earlier than usual, they made their way down to the shore of Lake Harney and set off in the small, wooden boat that they kept chained to a tree on the beach for easy launch. The old Mercury motor sprang to life and they were on their way as dawn broke. The lake was rough but white caps were not yet forming by the time they reached their trap line on the far side of the lake. As they pulled in each of the traps they noticed that the water was becoming rougher. The wind had picked up and the temperature was dropping rapidly. They discussed whether or not to leave the remaining traps unattended, but decided to finish like they did twice each week. It was a bad decision.

By the time they had pulled the last trap, the wind was roaring, the lake was white capping and they were shivering. In the bottom of the boat was a good catch and the money would help with two extra mouths to feed. Dad cranked the motor and headed the little boat toward the beach landing across the lake. Water began occasionally breaking over the bow of the boat and Vernon bailed constantly. The waves now were getting larger but both men continued on in stoic silence, Vernon bailing, Dad steering. When they were within three hundred yards of their destination the boat could take no more of the pounding water. Near the bow of the boat, a board separated from the forward spline and they were now helpless as the water rushed in. Bailing was out of the question. The boat was sinking in the water.

Neither man had a life jacket as it was an expense not in the budget. Vernon had never told dad that he could not swim but it now was time to confess. Dad was stunned by the revelation of his friend. The boat flipped over in the rough water, the motor broke loose and sank, and both men were hanging on to the boat. It was only thing that might save either of them. Because the board that failed was high, near the gunnel, the overturned boat had an air pocket trapped under it. It kept the boat afloat. Their fear was that the waves might flip the boat right side up and it would sink. Both men were cold with no other choice but to hang on to the boat. The hours dragged by and they wondered when the wind might blow them to shore.

At home, Iona became worried when the two men had not returned by midday. They should have been back for lunch before taking their catch to sell to the fish wholesale house in Sanford. By two o'clock she walked to a neighbor's house and asked to use their phone to call the Sheriff's office. Uniformed men came and took details from her, but after surveying the lake, told her that they had no boat at their disposal that would be safe for a search party. They told her that the two men were probably lost and that they would start a search for their bodies when the storm abated. It was now near sunset. Iona was stunned.

The storm raged on through the night. Sometimes there was light rain, but the cold, high winds were the storms main signature. Hope was running out in the house by the orange grove. We feared that we would never see either man again.

At eight o'clock the next morning a car pulled up to the house and out stepped Dad and Vernon. They were haggard and wearing different clothes than those they worn when they left the day before. We all ran to hug them. They only wanted to go to bed. The uniformed men came later that day and were surprised that both men were home. They talked to Dad and Vernon, made notes, then left.

The storm passed the next day. Now fully recovered, Vernon and Dad told us the whole story. Each time the wind would blow the overturned boat nearer the shore, the wind changed directions and blew them out to deeper water. Exhausted, Vernon had twice lost his grip on the boat and my father had pulled him back to safety. They encouraged one another to hang on and not give up. It was dark and the hours dragged on with each man getting weaker. The water was warmer than the air or hypothermia would have killed them by now. Finally, their luck changed.

Like many lakes in Florida, Lake Harney is a shallow lake. Sometime after midnight and before dawn, Dad realized that he was near enough to the shore that he could hold his breath, go under the boat, extend his arms and walk on the bottom of the lake dragging the boat and Vernon with him. When they finally dragged the boat up on the beach they collapsed on the sand and slept. They used the boat to shield them from the wind while they slept. When they awoke, they had no idea where they were. At dawn they walked along the sparsely populated lake shore until they found a house. The owner heard their story, gave them clean, dry clothes to wear and his wife cooked breakfast. They had not eaten in twenty-four hours. After breakfast he drove them home.

It had been a miracle that either man had survived. Vernon said that he would have perished if not for Dad's rescues and constant encouragement while in the water. Dad now needed a new boat and motor. Vernon never went back on the water and moved out a few months later.

CHAPTER TEN

THE MEAN SUMMER

It took Dad a few weeks to locate another boat. He had returned to the one left on the beach but decided that it was beyond repair. The boat that he chose was nearly identical to the one that he lost. Made of wood, the second-hand boat was about 17 feet long with a heavy coat of green paint and wooden bench seats, fore and aft. The motor was also used. There was no trailer, but Dad had prevailed on a couple of friends to help him load the boat onto the skeeter and haul it to the lake, where it was chained to a tree at the water's edge.

Easter came early that year on March 23, 1951. Dad now had five mouths to feed, and although Vernon was still with us he made clear that he would not fish again. Income had become a problem that they needed to solve quickly.

Palm Sunday provided a temporary solution. Churches need palms for the holy services that celebrate Jesus' return to Jerusalem. Dad learned that a dealer in Sanford bought fronds from local cutters and retailed them to churches across the country. The large prairies along the St. Johns River were thick with cabbage palms and land owners allowed those who asked, to harvest the central frond. Dad and Vernon bought palm axes and went to work. They worked long hard hours trying to meet the fast approaching deadline set by the market. They were paid eighty dollars per thousand fronds and it was enough to temporarily keep us afloat.

On the first trip out in his new boat, Dad emptied the traps of dead and live fish, baited them and returned the traps to the water. He was fishing again. Now that Vernon was no longer helping him the larger number of traps was hard to handle. On the days when traps were heavy with catfish it was hard to pull them over the gunnel of the boat. The chicken wire cut his fingers and the work and water made healing slow. Gloves were too clumsy for the mesh of the wire.

By the time he ran the traps, returned to shore, drove to Sanford and cleaned his catch for the buyer, he was exhausted. He began stopping at a bar for a drink and a rest period before heading home. One drink turned to two and soon his drinking became a problem again.

On April 11, 1951, President Truman relieved General of the Army Douglas MacArthur of his command for making statements that contradicted the administration\s policy. The war had started a year earlier on June 25, 1950 when North Korean troops had invaded the south. General MacArthur had been chosen to lead the United Nations sanctioned conflict.

Dad was outraged. He had served under General MacArthur in the Second World War, and he felt strongly that MacArthur had saved many soldier's lives with his brilliant wartime strategic moves. MacArthur was widely revered by his troops and Dad was no exception. "That son of a bitch, Truman, ought to be thrown out of office. MacArthur is a hero. What the hell has Truman ever done?" He seemed to have forgotten that it was President Truman who ordered the dropping of the atom bombs that ended the war in the Pacific. He raged on for days.

By May, Dad's dark memories began to creep in once again and now the water was warming and algae was forming on the traps. The catches diminished. By June he had hauled up the traps and they were drying in the yard. The catches were not paying for the bait.

Vernon now realized that he needed to move on. He left without giving an indication of where he was going.

There was now very little income and Dad was drinking

more often. Iona's meals became meager as she had little money with which to feed the family. Beans and rice became the norm. We ate the few oranges that the pickers had missed when they harvested the grove in March. Dad occasionally killed a rabbit. Once for a few days, Iona, Dad and I were reduced to one meal a day. I ate a lot of shriveled oranges from the trees in the grove. Eddie and Denise got their full allotment of food.

Finally, Dad decided that he needed to try using a trot line to catch enough fish to pay the bills and for the first time I was a part of his plans. I was ready to join his world and to earn his respect. Little did I know what was in store that summer.

Trot lines consist of a series of short fish lines with hooks, attached to a strong central line that can be strung across a body of water. Our line had a hundred or more hooks. Each hooked line hung down fifteen inches below the central line and were spaced at thirty six inch intervals. When not being used, they were carefully wound in circular rows in wash tubs to dry and avoid tangling. It was an art that Dad quickly mastered, making it easy to set or take in the line

Unlike trapping, where traps were visited each Saturday and Wednesday, trot- lining had a demanding schedule that required much greater commitment. Our week started on Sunday. Shortly after the noon meal, Dad would take me to the lake and drop me off with two galvanized wash tubs. He then returned home to load the motor and other provisions.

I would take one tub and float it by my side while wading in the shallow water. Being barefoot I could feel the fresh water mussels with my toes, then reach down, pick them up and place them in the tub. They were not hard to find and I was expected to find a few hundred over the next two hours. When one tub was filled to a level that it was in danger of sinking I switched to the second tub. When Dad returned at three o'clock, he expected to find all of the mussels that we would need for bait that week.

If there were not enough mussels in the tubs he would take off his shoes and help me finish, but I would get a bit of his scorn while we finished our task. "Damn it boy. What were you doing for the last two hours?" I quickly learned that failure was not an option and became proficient at finding the required amount. Before we left the boat landing, we shucked out a large coffee can of muscles to let them begin to sour. Catfish would eat soured mussels but sunfish, which we did not want, were more selective. By letting them sour we could conserve bait.

Loading the gear that we would need for the next four days into the boat only required a few minutes. Our gear consisted of muscles for bait, trot line, several one-gallon bottles of water, a wooden box of cooking supplies, two fish cars and a tarp. Next came the motor, gas, paddles and a tool box. Finally we would be off on our journey, me in the front seat, Dad in the back, the wind in our face like some grand adventure.

Out on the lake Dad turned the nose of the boat south toward the mouth of the St. Johns River, which lay two and a half miles from the launching point. A mile further down river we passed under the highway 46 bridge and Geiger's Fish Camp, where we had lived in the summer of 1949. Another mile beyond the bridge lay the entrance to our destination, the Econlockhatchee River. Now the going was slow. The shallow, serpentine river ran through a mile and a half of marsh grass mud flats before reaching the timberline. Fallen trees washed out in storms were just below the surface of the water and represented a hazard to the motor. My job was to lean over the bow of the little boat and point out submerged obstacles. When I failed, Dad would bump into the underwater obstacle, causing the cotter pin that held the propeller to the motor's shaft to break, and the propeller would stop turning. Dad would then raise the motor and replace the broken pin before continuing on our journey. Comments about my eyesight and attentiveness accompanied the repair.

Once in the timberline, the river deepened and the water

was clear but stained dark from tannin. Sunken trees remained a navigation problem for the next mile or two until we reached a sandy spot on the shoreline where we set up camp. Our camp was primitive. We slept on top of the tarp unless it rained, or the mosquitoes were too severe. Both were problems. Dad cooked our meals in a frying pan over an open wood fire. If we ran out of the drinking water that we had brought, we drank creek water. He had survived the horrible conditions of the war in the Philippines and never seemed uncomfortable with our fate that summer. I scratched chigger and mosquito bites every day.

Upon arrival at our campsite, we unloaded the gear except for the bait and trot line, then began the process of setting the line in the river. The trot line was strung back and forth across the river until all of it was out of the tubs. We then set about baiting the hooks. Dad sat in the front seat and I in the back. My job was to keep the boat at the proper angle so that the line would pass over the boat at a forty five degree angle while Dad was baiting hooks. Later when we came back to check our catch, my job was the same, but this time Dad would take off the fish and bait the hook before returning the line to the water. We always kept an inch or two of water in the bottom of the boat so that the fish were alive when we returned to camp. Dad would then put the fish in a fish car made of chicken wire to keep them alive until Thursday, when we returned home. We ran the traps three times a day, with one run being at night. Dad used a battery powered head light for the night run. The monotony of night runs made it difficult for me to stay alert in the back of the boat. I had no light and few bearings, but was expected to keep the boat on a proper course so that Dad could efficiently drag the line across the bow of the boat. When I failed at this, Dad would growl "Wake up boy! If you don't keep this damn boat straight, I'm gonna throw you in the creek and let that big alligator eat you!" His admonition was often accompanied by a tin can of creek water, thrown at me from the bow of the boat. I never thought that he would throw me over, but I was still a little nervous about the possibility. We saw the big ten-foot gator almost every time that we made the trip up river and he always looked menacing. Trot lining was hard work and our living conditions were miserable.

On Thursday morning we retrieved the trot line, packed up our camp gear, loaded the fish cars, and our catch, before returning to the boat landing where Dad had left the skeeter. The fish were kept alive in the bottom of the boat by adding an inch of water in the boat to keep their gills wet. He stopped at the house to drop me and the gear off and grab a sandwich before heading to Sanford. At the fish house he still had to skin and clean the fish in order to wholesale them to the owner/broker. By late afternoon he would return tired, disheveled, hungry and with a couple bottles of Four Roses whiskey. On the weekends the dark moods returned and they were getting worse.

By late July we were not going trot lining every week. It was taking a toll on Dad and so was the alcohol. He and Iona argued about the amount of money that he spent on whiskey, but he never hit her like he had my mother. Things were at a low point in our house and he often took out his anger on Eddie and me. He would beat Eddie with his belt almost daily for the smallest of infractions. Although I also was familiar with the belt and his berating me, it was nothing like Eddie endured. Iona would cry and beg him to stop but he seldom did.

Late one morning in early August Dad could not get the skeeter to start. Already a drink or two into the day he had skinned his knuckles with the hand crank, and cussed the car thoroughly, before calling me out from the house. He told me that he had a friend that was a shade tree mechanic that could fix the car. I was to fetch him.

My directions to find his friend were to go to the lake and walk to the right along the lake shore until I found the second white frame house on the lakes edge. I left right away and began following his directions. Summer rains had filled the lake and it was difficult to make my way along the lakes edge. The Cypress knees in the water were a problem and the water was forbidding in places among the cypress. I imagined snakes and maybe a gator might be among the knees now covered with dark water. Nevertheless, I continued on until I ran into a wide creek that flowed into the lake. Summer rains had caused the water in the creek to move swiftly. I started to wade, but the water in the creek quickly rose to my neck. I then tried to swim the creek and the current began carrying me out into the lake. I panicked and returned to the creek bank. I was not a strong swimmer, but tried once more with the same results. Finally, I decided to return home. I had failed and I knew that Dad would be mad.

When I walked up on the porch Dad was waiting for me. He had seen me from a distance, and I could tell that he was angry. He demanded to know why I had come back without the help that he needed. I relayed what had happened at the creek and he became enraged, asking me to repeat the story again and again. With each telling he became more incensed. He smelled of whiskey. Finally he ordered me to sit on the top step of the porch. He took his belt off and I knew that I was in for it. I sat there and took the lashes, crying as little as possible. The belt stung but I had felt that before. Now the words cut deeper. He kept repeating "I never thought that I would raise a coward. You are a coward. A coward is what you are." When he finally had vented his frustration with the longest whipping that I had ever experienced, he ordered me to remain on the top step and went in to the house.

I sat there in the August sun for about thirty minutes before Iona came out to check on me. My father had apparently gone to bed and she now felt that it was safe for her to come out. I was wearing a white cotton tee shirt that she gingerly lifted to see what needed to be done. The shirt was mixed with sweat and a small amount of blood and lymph fluid. As she removed the shirt, it stuck to my back. Iona then went to the well, drew a basin of water and washed my wounds with a cloth. Next she applied alcohol which really stung and told me to sit in a chair in the shade with no shirt to let the wounds dry.

That night at supper, Dad said not a word to me or the other kids and very few to Iona. After the dishes had been washed and dried, Iona blew out the kerosene lamps and we all went to bed.

I awoke the next morning with Dad standing next to my cot. He handed me a paper bag and said for me to put my clothes in it. At breakfast he was silent. Once we had eaten, he told me to get in the skeeter and to bring my clothes. I had no idea where we were going. The skeeter's engine started on the second spin of the crank. Dad said not a word on the trip, and I knew better than to ask. When we finally stopped, he told me to stay in the skeeter before walking up to the living quarters, where he knocked on the door and entered. I did not know it then, but I would never again live with my father.

CHAPTER ELEVEN

REFUGE IN INDIAN RIVER CITY

Soon after we arrived, Dad and an older man walked into the back yard and stood talking in low voices. Their conversation lasted a half hour or more. While they talked, I sat in the skeeter. After a while, a short, rotund woman with white hair came to the front door and motioned for me to come inside. Once inside, she made small talk, and then offered me a piece of cake and a cup of coffee. I accepted her kind generosity. It was the first coffee that I had drunk in a long time.

When the two men finished talking, they came in and Dad said, "Get your clothes. You're staying here with your grandfather." He then said his goodbyes to his father and Grandma Jimmy and followed me to the skeeter. When I had retrieved my paper bag of clothes, he cranked up the skeeter, put it in gear, and drove away down the narrow dirt path that would take him back to Geneva. My father never said goodbye to me, nor did he look back. He wanted nothing more to do with me.

Although I had twice met Grandpa Will before the war, I did not recognize him or Grandma Jimmy. They now were in their mid-sixties and in poor health. Both had diabetes. Grandpa was a handsome man, maybe five foot ten inches tall and a hundred seventy pounds. His hair was white with natural streaks of yellow. He shaved twice a week so that he usually had a stubble beard. He liked to tell stories in his gravelly voice.

Grandma Jimmy was a short, stout woman with a small

high-pitched voice and a big heart. Like Grandpa Will, she had been married before and had a son named Quinn who dropped by periodically to check on them. After Dad was gone, I was shown to where I would sleep.

My new residence was in an old yellow school bus whose seats had been removed. It no longer had tires but it had been jacked up and cross ties placed under to support the frame. Inside there were two beds. One bed was a standard double bed at the back of the bus and the other was a single bed placed behind where the driver's seat would have been. Will and Jimmy had lived in the bus until she became so heavy that it became hard for her to climb the steps.

While I slept in the bus, they had fashioned an adjacent place for them to live. A few years earlier Grandpa Will had poured a concrete slab the length of the bus's seating area and ten feet wide. The walls were constructed of slab wood obtained free from a near-by sawmill and the building had a tin roof. Ventilation was achieved by raising the two slab-wood shutters that covered four by six feet window openings in the wall opposite the bus. One opening was above their bed and the other was beside the stove. The openings were screened to keep out insects but had no glass. In the summer the shutters were raised and the windows were kept open day and night. In the winter, translucent plastic was attached over the out-side of the openings to let in the light. A door was at each end of the structure. A small table for eating was just big enough for the three of us and there were two small chest-of-drawers for storing their clothing. A small wood stove provided both heat in winter and was used for everyday cooking. In August the heat from the stove was unbearable, but Grandma Jimmy never missed preparing a meal.

A hand pump for drawing water stood no more than twenty feet from the back door and a small wooden platform was placed in front of the pump, so that you could bathe and not have to stand in the sand. The outhouse was approximately fifty feet from the bus. Needless to say there was no electricity.

The day I arrived was hot and muggy, and the heat in both buildings soon became very uncomfortable. It was like that every day in the summer. The windows on the bus could be opened during the day but had to be closed long before dark to keep out mosquitoes.

Grandpa Will and Grandma Jimmy had developed a routine to deal with the heat, and now I was a part of that routine. At four o'clock each day, Grandpa Will would crank up his skeeter and we would head in to a small grocery store in Indian River City. Grandpa's skeeter was exactly like the one Dad drove. Will and Jimmy would sit up front, and I and their big black and tan dog, Trigger, would ride on the bed of the vehicle. It did not take long for me and Trigger to become friends. Trigger was Grandpa's cow dog, and maybe he needed a boy about as much as I needed a dog at that time in my life.

When we arrived at the grocery store every afternoon, despite having diabetes, Grandpa Will bought a quart of beer and Grandma Jimmy got a pint of ice cream. They bought me ice cream on a stick. Grandma Jimmy would buy enough food for supper and for the next day. It was their social time as they sat enjoying talking to people who frequented the store. They were regulars as were several others. I would go across the street and walk along the Indian River hoping to catch a glimpse of mullet jumping and other treasures. Trigger would not leave the skeeter.

After an hour or so the weather would start to cool and we returned to Grandpa's humble abode. Grandma Jimmy would fire up the wood stove and cook our supper. Our living quarters would not cool down before nine PM in August and early September. The tin roof and the school bus retained the heat long after the sun had set.

Grandpa Will's place was located three miles west of Indian River City. It was located in a small triangle of land whose boundaries were highway 50, state road 405 and a small paved access road connecting the two. Uncle Leon owned a hundred and sixty acres of land on the opposite side of the highway. He had bought the property for taxes after the war and it was said that he paid $4.60 per acre. The land was unimproved with large swatches of Spartina that only could be eaten by cattle when it was recently burned off to let tender new shoots emerge. He and his brother, Grandpa Will, had an agreement about the care of the cattle. Grandpa Will looked after the cattle every few days because Uncle Leon lived in Kissimmee. Uncle Leon came every few weeks and did whatever fence repair and other ranch work that was necessary. In the winter he brought citrus molasses in fifty-gallon drums to supplement the cattle's limited grazing. In return for Will's services, Uncle Leon provided a modest income for his older brother.

In the summer of 1951, mosquito populations were heavy. They came in droves forcing Uncle Leon's cattle to move constantly at night. We built smudge fires out of wood that Grandpa Will had piled up the previous winter, and freshly cut green wax myrtle. The small fires formed clouds of smoke that gave the cattle some relief. Back at our living quarters we did the same because the bus and their quarters were too hot until a couple of hours after the sun had set. When the bus finally cooled down I would bathe by the pump and turn in for the evening. Occasionally the mosquito control plane would fly over and we sat out as the insecticidal mist drifted down upon us, completely oblivious to the possible consequences. We always smelled of smoke.

Grandpa Will was a great story teller and as we sat in the smoke he entertained Grandma Jimmy and me with stories of growing up in Florida during the first quarter of the century. She had her own stories too. She had been a work-camp cook earlier in life and had experienced hard times, like everyone who lived through the depression. When Uncle Leon stayed over, the stories were even more wonderful. It was evident that the two men were close.

In addition to their stories, they still had a little of that sibling rivalry that most brothers have. On three visits, Uncle Leon and Grandpa Will had pistol shooting contests. Both had 410 pistols that were useful as saddle guns. The single shot weapons had a pistol grip with a barrel that was about sixteen inches long. Its ammunition was 410 shotgun shells. They would line up targets and take turns until one had bested the other. Then the victor would laugh and the loser would vow to get even the next time. It was great fun for a twelve year old boy to watch them.

When September came, they took me to Titusville and enrolled me in the seventh grade. School was an ordinary experience but time spent with Will and Jimmy was special. We checked the cattle, piled wood for the next summer's smudge fires, and tended a little pineapple patch that they had planted in the hammock across the highway. Grandma Jimmy loved pineapples and I checked the patch almost daily that summer to try to find a ripe one. Everywhere that Grandpa went, he took Trigger and me. They each were kind and generous with what they had to share, but they probably were too old for this new responsibility.

Shortly before Christmas, Grandma Jimmy's son, Quinn Melvin and his wife, moved into the bus with me. He was out of work with no prospects on the horizon. My presence in the bus was awkward for the married couple who had no privacy. It was clear that my time in Indian River City was rapidly coming to an end.

CHAPTER TWELVE

RETURN TO KISSIMMEE: HOECAKES AND AMBROSIA

A few days after school let out for Christmas Break in 1951, Uncle Leon showed up for one of his visits. He did not stay long. He had come to take me home to Kissimmee. My mother was now back from Orlando and I had a new three-month old baby sister. Her name was Jo Marie. It was not clear if Mom had wanted me to come help her, or if Will and Jimmy, having done all that could have been expected, wanted their old lives back again.

After lunch I put my paper bag of clothes in the truck and we headed out for Kissimmee. On the way back we stopped at at the town of Christmas to get a five-gallon bottle of sulfur water from an artesian well along the road. Uncle Leon always stopped at this well and filled his bottle to take back because he was convinced that the water had healing qualities. The trip was otherwise uneventful. He periodically burst in to song to pass the time and he asked me how my visit had been. I told him that the time with Grandpa Will and Grandma Jimmy had been great. He already knew the rest of the story.

Upon her return, Mom had rented a small two room apartment in a private home at the intersection of Emmett Street and Limit Street. She, Denise, and Jo Marie shared the bedroom and I slept on the couch in the small room that served as kitchen, eating area and living room.

We celebrated Christmas in that apartment with a small sand pine tree, courtesy of Uncle Leon. There were very few presents. We pretended that Jo Marie in her crib was the baby Jesus and then laughed. We rang in the New Year of 1952 the next week with little fanfare.

Mom had already begun working at the crate mill again, and I now had increased responsibilities to help her in our home. She had been taking Denise, who had turned four years old in the summer of 1951 and the baby to a sitter about three hundred yards further down the road toward the former military base. The sitter was paid by the hour and Mom could not get home from the mill until almost six o'clock, because she had no car. After paying the sitter she had little left for all of her effort at the mill. The apartment was located on the opposite side of Limit Street from where we had previously lived and I now rode the bus to school, allowing me to arrive home by four each afternoon. I went immediately to the sitter's home and collected my sisters and the baby bottles and dirty diapers in order to save two hours of sitter fees. I slung the bag of bottles and diapers over my shoulder, carried Jo Marie and held Denise by the hand as we walked down the sand road toward the apartment. It must have been quite a sight!

After a few months we were able to move out of the crowded little apartment and have some space. Our new home was just down the street. It was the house that Mom and Dad had owned when they were married. The people who now owned it had renovated it into a rental duplex. I immediately felt at home, and the Farmer family on the other side had kids who became my friends. Our side of the duplex had a living room, two bedrooms, a kitchen with an eating area and a large back porch. Both families shared the large front porch. On our side we had a large guava patch which soon became important to our well-being. When the guavas were ripe we picked bushels of them and a friend of Mom's hauled them to the Jelly Factory on North Main Street. Guavas became an important source of our family's supplemental income.

Although I was now living with Mom, Dad's presence soon

reentered our lives. One afternoon a car with a couple of men pulled into our yard, and one of them got out and asked for my mother. Mom recognized him, but I did not. The man asked if we knew where Uncle Leon was because he was not at home. He quickly explained that Dad had been shot and was in Lancaster's Hospital. The bleeding had been stopped, but because Dad had no cash with him, the hospital wanted proof of payment before performing surgery. Dad had asked the men to find Uncle Leon to guarantee payment.

Dad had been shot twice, once in the leg and once in the hand. Neither wound was life threatening but needed immediate medical care. He had been shot by his brother-in-law, Roy Bacon. Roy was the husband of Dad's sister, Iris. They had argued and Dad became threatening, so Roy, being a smaller man, pulled a gun. I do not believe that charges were ever filed.

Mom explained that she was not sure, but suggested that Uncle Leon usually checked his cattle on Sunday afternoon. I knew where his cattle were pastured on Vineland Road near Shingle Creek. The man said, "Get in and show me where this pasture is." Mom quickly added, "Go and help find Uncle Leon."

When we got near the pasture entrance, I could see the old Ford cattle truck in the distance and pointed it out. The driver pulled in but Uncle Leon was nowhere to be seen. I jumped out of the car and began running as fast as I could through the piney woods. I was not wearing shoes and the ground was rough under my feet. Palmettos scratched my arms and legs. Uncle Leon pastured his cattle on a large piece of land owned by Irlo Bronson. Uncle Leon earlier had been a line foreman for Mr. Bronson in the days when cattle were pastured on open range. In gratitude, Irlo had rented the pastureland to Uncle Leon at a good price.

I was quickly realizing just how big the property was when I spied him on his horse in the distance. My brother Leon was not with him on this Sunday which struck me as odd. I ran faster and began yelling, "Uncle Leon, Dad's been shot." He began riding toward me. When we came closer, I was out of breath but relayed the story as fast as I could.

"Give me your hand," he said in a loud voice as he reached down toward me. We joined hands at the wrists and with one swift motion of his left hand he pulled me up behind him on his horse and said, "Hold on". We galloped through the woods, dodging pine trees and palmetto patches, and I held on for dear life.

Back at the truck we loaded the horse, drove into town, and parked at the hospital. He strode in the front door and to the rear of the hospital, with me in close pursuit. He demanded in a loud voice from the first nurse he saw to know where Dad was. She pointed down the hall. We walked into the room where Dad was on a gurney outside of the operating room. He had blood-soaked bandages on his hand and thigh. He had been given first aid and pain medicine. Taking one look at the startled nurse on duty Uncle Leon bellowed, "I'll pay for it. Take him back." Dad promptly disappeared behind two swinging doors. I stood in awe of the power Uncle Leon had with people and also to the power of money. Uncle Leon then told me that he would stay with Dad and that I was to walk home as it was getting dark and Mom would be worried.

Dad recovered from his wounds, but his hand was permanently crippled, further complicating his life. Work would now be harder to find. He had escaped the war without a scratch, but now had been wounded by a relative in civilian life. He had another reason to be depressed.

A month or so after moving back to Limit Street, Mom had a gentleman caller and began dating again. There were others, but none lasted long enough for me to remember their names. Only one became a regular beau and he was someone that I really liked. His name was Gordon Lee (last name withheld to protect his descendants privacy). Gordon regularly brought

Denise and me treats and talked with us before they went out for their date. I hoped that he and Mom would be married, but that was not to be.

In August, 1952, Mom told me that she was pregnant. I jumped to conclusions and asked if she and Gordon were getting married. She teared up and said no. He had not told her that he was already married. I was crushed. Hard times were again knocking on Mom's door and there was no place for her to turn for help.

Mom continued working at the mill until she began showing. Whether they laid her off or she concluded that she needed to quit to protect the baby was unclear. What was clear was that Gordon was out of the picture, and she had no visible means of support.

Uncle Leon stepped up deliveries of eggs, chickens, and meat scraps. Aunt Betty delivered a basket of food and my mother cried knowing that she was no longer able to manage without help. She began to take in washing to feed us. Where she got the money for rent was a mystery.

I fished, picked up pop bottles along the roads for the two-cent deposit, picked and sold wild blackberries door to door. For my mid-day meal, I scraped plates in the lunchroom. When my soles separated from my shoes that year I wired them back together with baling wire which drew more attention from the other kids than I was seeking. On a few occasions Mom was down to hardly anything to eat and she sometimes made hoecakes and ambrosia for supper. She fried a mixture of flour and water in lard and sent me out into the night to appropriate a few oranges from a neighbor's small grove. It always seemed funny to me that Mom had a small bag of sweetened coconut shreds, when other food supplies were scarce. The bag was probably left over from better times. The mixture of oranges and coconut washed down the hoecake and we went to bed with full bellies and high hopes for better times.

David Lee Allen arrived on January 30, 1953, and

immediately created a mystery that was not exposed until many years later. His birth certificate showed that Ralph Carl Allen was listed as his father. Mom and Dad had gone through a bitter divorce four years before David's birth. They were cordial, but not particularly good friends. Mom went to her grave without ever explaining, and David never knew this until he found his birth certificate after Mom died on April 29, 1976. I suspect that she did this to protect his married father and because she retained her married name of Allen. Sometimes one has to swallow their pride and act in the interest of the newly born. Although I have no proof, I always assumed that Gordon was the father.

Once she recovered from giving birth, Mom went back to toiling at the mill. But she began feeling arthritis in her hands and feet and it was getting harder to run the machines at the mill. She was on her feet all day and then had to walk home. Her health was becoming a problem.

We still picked guavas for the Esper Jelly Factory and she made jelly and guava butter for our consumption. Her guava butter on biscuits or hoecake was exceptional. I have bought guava butter several times as an adult but it is always a disappointment.

The Jelly factory created tropical jellies and related products from fruit like those we sold to them. Their products were sold to tourist shops and cruise ships in "Welcome Baskets" under the trade name Esper Products. A member of the business community for more than fifty years, it now is closed.

Mom began seeing Walter Alderman in the spring of 1953. They seemed happy together right from the beginning.

CHAPTER THIRTEEN

AULTMAN ISLAND: UNDER THE MANGO TREE

By early summer 1953, we moved again, this time to Aultman Island off Neptune Road. The old house was in the center of the island where Brownie Wise County Park now stands. Our new home had once been a fine middle-class house but was showing its age. The entire island had been cleared many years earlier for farming but now served only as grazing land. Plez (Last name withheld to protect the privacy of his decendants), a local cattleman served as the caretaker for the island. He had responsibility for the cattle and the house. A wooden bridge and a dirt road connected Aultman Island to that part of Cypress Island where my grandfather, Albert King, had raised Mom and her six siblings. The dirt road continued on to Aunt Ruth's house at the intersection with Neptune Road.

Mr. Aultman had purchased the island in 1923. The sale was carried in the May 27, 1923 edition of the Tampa Tribune.

"Fifteen Thousand Dollars Paid For Eighteen Acres Fertile Cypress Island"

The first week in May, this year, W.H. Wilcox sold to S.B. AULTMAN of Kissimmee eighteen acres of his rich Cypress Island Holdings for $15,000.

Cypress Island is two miles from Kissimmee in Lake Tohopakaliga a rich prairie myrtle soil and capable of high cultivation. On the eighteen acres transferred by this sale is a seven acre grove of twelve year old orange trees in fine condition and annually

producing a large pack of the best quality fruit. On the place two flowing artesian wells supply water for the trucking industry, which is carried on.

Allowing a thousand dollars an acre for the seven acre orange grove--- which is recognized as a fair and common price for good groves---that leaves eleven thousand dollars as the price paid for the other eight acres of land in the transfer---a price of record for trucking lands, untiled, even in Florida. Although the inherent possibilities of the place warrant the belief that after the place is prepared for intensive farm operations the net yield from each or any acre will more than pay in one year the price paid per acre."

The house had electricity, indoor plumbing, and running water made possible by an electric pump connected to an artesian well. The well was located at the back of the house under a large mango tree. The artesian well flowed continuously but had been plumbed to yield to the electric pump. The water was cool and sweet and when we were hot from being outside we all drank directly from the well using a tin cup that hung on a nail in the trunk of the mango tree. After we drank our fill, we often dipped our heads under the cascading water or poured the water over our bodies to cool off.

There was a large screened back porch, a small screened front porch, three bedrooms, a large eat-in kitchen, and a living room. Because the two porches were screened the house could be left open to capture lake breezes.

An old wooden barn was near the house, and small fenced pens for livestock were attached to the barn. The pens needed repair but Mom had no livestock other than the dozen chickens that Uncle Leon brought on his first visit. After he brought the chickens, his delivery of eggs and meat scraps stopped because our house was substantially out of his normal driving pattern. He also did not like Mom's new boyfriend, Walter.

In addition to the big mango tree by the well, there was a

smaller mango tree by the house and another two down by the lake. A few dozen scraggly orange trees were all that was left from the 42 year-old grove, but they produced a small crop of fruit in the cold months.

Mom still had no car. She walked to Aunt Ruth's house each morning to catch a ride to the crate mill where both women worked. She continued to work at the mill even though her hands were showing signs of advancing rheumatoid arthritis.

Ruth and Henry lived at the intersection of Aultman Road and Neptune Road. In bad weather Ruth picked Mom up in her pickup truck and brought her home each evening. I spent the summer caring for my three siblings so that she could work. By now I was veteran bottle warmer and diaper changer.

To pass the time, I listened to the radio that Mom bought. It was there that I heard that the Korean War had ended with an armistice on July 27, 1953. Almost 36, 000 American soldiers had died along with countless Allied, Korean and Chinese troops. The toll on civilians was staggering. In the end, the South Koreans were still sovereign and the border with North Korea was little changed. I wondered how many families had been ruined by the war. The Military Demarcation Line remains one of the most militarized zones in the world.

In August 1953, Walter moved in with us. He was separated from his wife and waiting for his final divorce papers. There were now two incomes though neither earned more than one dollar an hour. It was the first time that Mom had not been the sole bread winner and she liked it. Both of them now shared expenses and responsibilities. They planned for the future together even as they both knew that Mom's health might get worse. Walter was at ease with Mom's younger children, and later adopted them. Walter and I had a different relationship. It was always a little edgy and we were never close, even though we both tried.

Walter was a short, slightly rotund man with thinning

brown hair, which he slicked back over the top of his head. He wore cotton, short-sleeved shirts and khaki pants. A wide-brimmed straw hat and work boots completed his wardrobe.

He laughed easily and Mom liked his humor. He had not finished high school and once indicated to me that he had not gone beyond third grade. He worked as a laborer when he could find work and he used an old flat-bed truck to haul things for other people. At heart, Walter was a trader. He liked buying something and trying to make a buck by selling it for more money. He was good at trading because he had honed exaggeration and self-promotion to a high art. With Walter it was always "Buyer beware."

Soon after Walter moved in he, Mom, Ruth, and Henry bought a newly-fresh Jersey milk cow. The little Jersey cow produced lots of creamy rich milk every morning and again in the evening. Mom and Ruth shared the milk. Ruth bought sweet feed and milked the cow after work and Mom milked her in the morning. In between milking, the cow grazed in open pasture. Both families had all of the milk, cream and home-made butter we needed. Churning butter soon became one of my responsibilities.

My younger cousin Bruce, who was Ruth and Henry's son, was my primary companion that summer. When I was not minding my siblings, he and I fished and explored the waterfront of the island looking for whatever critters were hiding in the water hyacinth beds at the edge of the lake. Once we found a small wooden boat partially submerged in the hyacinths. It had probably drifted there after breaking loose in a storm, and the owners had given up looking for it. After finding the boat we went home to retrieve shovels to dig it out of the mud. We told Walter what we had found, and he joined us in the recovery. Once out of the muck, we all hauled it up on the shore and turned it over to inspect the bottom. Walter told us to let it dry for a couple of weeks before we tried to put it back in the water.

When it came time to try out the boat, Walter took Mom out on the lake for a fishing trip. There were no oars but Lake Tohopekaliga is a shallow lake and a long stout pole was enough to propel the little boat out to a large bed of Bonnet Lilies where they caught enough blue gills for supper. They had taken no bait with them but had caught fish. I asked how they did this but Walter only laughed and said that it was a secret. He later showed me how, and I learned a new trick about fishing.

They had used Bonnet worms. Bonnet Lilies have a moth that lays an egg at the junction of the floating leaf pad and it's supporting stem. When the larva hatches it then bores into the stem to complete its life cycle. A single larva bores into and feeds on the interior of the stem. As it ingests the soft interior, the larva pushes its frass out of the stem, leaving it on the pad with a tell-tale hole. After Mom and Walter spied a pad with a hole in it they pulled it up, split the stem and used the larva for bait. It was a lesson that I have put to good use a great many times over the years.

That summer opportunity came knocking and I got my first chance to earn a paycheck. My brother chose me to help him clear land for planting grass. On work days he picked me up from the island in the 1950 Willys Jeep truck that belonged to Dr. Whaley. The work involved picking up stumps and pine roots, called "Lighter'd knots" by the locals, in preparation for planting new pasture land. The pine trees had been harvested for pulp wood leaving most of the stumps to be removed with a front end rake mounted on a bull dozer. While most of the stumps had been mechanically piled up and burned, there were still too many left to disc the land in preparation for planting.

Once at Dr. Whaley's ranch, Leon would drive the big John Deere Model R diesel tractor pulling a sled behind. I would walk along picking up stumps and large roots and placing them on the sled. When the sled was full, we would unload it and burn the stumps and roots. The work was hot, sweaty, and dirty. On two occasions I encountered a small eastern diamondback rattlesnake when I rolled over a big stump, and quickly jumped out of striking distance, much to Leon's amusement. Scorpions and bees were a more common but a less serious threat. Leather gloves were essential. The work only lasted for a couple of weeks, but I was happy to have some spending money.

That summer Leon used the Jeep to teach me to drive and I bumped all over the ranch's dirt roads at five to ten miles an hour. After obtaining my learners permit, Dr. Whaley finally gave me permission to practice driving on Boggy Creek Road under Leon's supervision.

On the day after Labor Day, at the age of fourteen, I began the ninth grade with a full load of math and science courses. I had learned the year before that those were my better subjects and I had a passion for them. I was anxious to catch the school bus every day and pleased to be in high school.

My brother Leon was a senior that year. He was President of the Student Body, in the Key Club and was a good high school athlete who had earned third team All-State honors as a football guard the previous year. A versatile athlete, he had also earned multiple letters for basketball, baseball, track and weight lifting. He was popular with everyone, especially the girls in school. He taught many of them to dance.

I had earlier tried to emulate him by going out for football in the eighth grade, but had little success, and later decided that football was not in my future. Unlike Leon, I was skinny as a rail and not built for contact. He assured me that I need not be concerned about my decision to give up the sport.

In previous years, when we were struggling financially, he had sometimes given me lunch money so that I did not have to scrape plates. He was always supportive, and I liked and admired him, as did most people.

In the spring of 1954, Walter decided to plant a cash crop to earn extra money. My Grandfather, Albert King, had raised

Mom and her siblings on the adjacent land by planting truck crops. Plez's cattle had been removed from the island in March, and Walter had someone come and plow up about an acre of ground for planting yellow crookneck summer squash and a few tomatoes. The crop flourished and provided plenty of weekends of hoeing for Mom, Walter and me. When the first squash was ready for picking, we were overwhelmed with bushels of the yellow vegetables. Walter and I loaded them on the flatbed truck and he took them to Orlando to sell to fruit and vegetable stands. He was successful with the first load of produce but squash ripens fast and we needed to pick every other day. It was not long before we had saturated the markets in Orlando and the surrounding towns and he had no other outlet for squash. Much of the squash that we picked was still on the truck when he returned at the end of the day. We suspended picking and the bushes, full of fruit, rotted in the field except for those we and our pig ate. Walter had produced a good crop but had failed to realize the limits of the market. In late May, Plez brought in a new crop of weaned calves to graze and was not happy to see that we had plowed up a piece of pasture land to plant squash. He and Walter had a heated discussion.

CHAPTER FOURTEEN

THE PARTING

The second day of summer vacation in June 1954 was the day that changed my life forever. The weather that morning was hot and sticky under a blue sky, punctuated with cumulus clouds. There was not a breath of air moving. The sun was an hour high when I awoke, rubbed the sleep from my eyes and smelled Mom's breakfast. The sheet was wet with my sweat and the dew that seeped in from the open window by my bed. It had rained the night before and the world was washed clean. In the nearby orange trees mockingbirds noisily sang as they wooed their gray and white feathered mates, and defended territory from rival males and other birds. Through my bedroom window, drifted the sounds and smells of cattle grazing in the pasture. It promised to be another stifling day on Aultman Island, the kind that makes your shirt stick to your back.-

I quickly dressed in faded jeans and a white, cotton, tee shirt. I slipped on my nearly worn out shoes bought new the previous September.

I ran water into a white metal basin and splashed it on my face. The water was not cold but it helped to wash the sleep from my eyes. After drying my face and hands, I walked into the kitchen where Mom was frying eggs and thick slices of bacon. A pot of grits bubbled on the three-burner kerosene stove and I could smell the biscuits baking in the oven. Standing at the stove, wearing a faded, blue print dress, Mom was making green tomato gravy in a cast iron skillet, stirring frequently to keep the gravy from burning. The gravy was special, made from bacon grease, flour and a few remaining, nearly-ripe tomatoes taken from plants in a patch near the front porch. She was the only person I ever knew that made this dish, but it was a family favorite. I later learned that it was a common dish in homes across the south. The full breakfast was my mother's way of helping ease the tension that was as heavy as the summer air.

"Hello Mama," I said while giving her a quick hug. She returned the greeting with a smile but continued stirring the gravy. There were too many things yet to be done, and she was feeling the need to finish cooking before Denise, Jo Marie, and Mike woke up. Mike had been born David Lee, but after Walter came to live with us the family started calling him Mike.

During the rain storm the previous evening, Mom and Walter had made us aware that they were going on a trip the next day, but there had been no attempt to share many details of their sudden departure. We only knew that they would be away for an extended period of time, at destinations unknown to anyone but themselves.

"Go help Walter load the truck while I finish breakfast," Mom said anxiously. I shuffled off to the back porch to carry cardboard boxes filled with my sister's and brother's clothes and a few toys to the truck. Later that morning Mom would strip the bed sheets, take the pillows and place them in boxes to be loaded with the others. Walter was busy arranging things on the truck when I carried out the first box. "Good morning Walter." "Well, I see that you finally woke up," he shot back in friendly banter. He then directed me to bring out the remainder of the boxes to the truck. The task only took a few minutes. I could hear the younger children waking up and went back inside to help dress them.

"Breakfast is ready," Mom called from the kitchen.

I hurried to finish washing the children's faces. Soon we were all seated around the old kitchen table eating grits, thick bacon strips, green tomato gravy, fried eggs and biscuits. The smaller children drank milk fresh from the cow Mom had milked soon after the sun had risen. There was a pot of strong, boiled coffee on the stove for the adults. I poured a cup of the brew, added too much milk, and washed down the last mouthful of biscuit and gravy.

A breakfast this good was not an everyday event. Over the last few months Walter had been finding fewer jobs and Mom's job at the mill had ended due to her advancing arthritis. Cash was scarce, but there was plenty of milk and enough eggs to supplement store-bought groceries. Mangoes were in season and we caught fish and shot wild rabbits. We also thinned the flock of chickens that Uncle Leon had brought when we first moved in. We were eating well but Mom and Walter were concerned about their financial future.

Denise who was now almost seven, was cranky and feeling apprehensive. She left her seat at the table and clung to Mom's neck. "When will you be back?" she inquired nervously.

"We don't know, but Aunt Ruth and Cousin Barbara will take good care of you," she replied in her most reassuring voice. Denise continued to cling to Mom but asked no more questions. The two younger children continued eating, oblivious to what was about to happen.

After breakfast, my mother washed the dishes, and then loaded all of the remaining food from an old well-worn cupboard into two, medium-sized wooden boxes. A few cooking utensils, flatware, plates and bowls were packed in similar manner. Walter and I carried them to the truck

"Have you packed your clothes?" Mom asked.

"Yes," I replied. "They are in a paper bag".

"Good," she called out. "Uncle Leon will pick you up later this morning. Walter has spoken with him and you can stay with him until we get back." I felt less concerned now that I knew Uncle Leon would be coming for me.

"When you leave, be sure to lock the door and put the key

under the well- stone," Walter instructed me. I never understood why we locked up because there was little of value left inside and the house was so isolated that anyone could break a window and get inside. Perhaps it was because there were so few items of value that it became even more important to protect the few beat-up chairs, the old kitchen table, and the rickety iron beds that numbered two fewer than the number of occupants.

Walter loaded a Coleman camp stove, bought new for the occasion, on the flat-bed Ford truck. Denise, Jo Marie, and Mike came next, each finding a place between Walter and the passenger door.

Mom hugged me and once again reassured me that Uncle Leon would soon be over to pick me up. With that she climbed into the passenger seat and closed the door. Everyone was calling "Good bye, good bye". Denise was crying softly. My mother was smiling and waving, and I was standing by the front gate, watching with uncertainty an all too familiar scene play out before me. Walter shifted the truck into gear and rumbled noisily toward the bridge that would take them off the island. The sideboards on the truck slapped rhythmically with each hole in the dirt ruts until the truck disappeared behind the wax myrtle trees that lined the road near the bridge. I watched and listened until I could neither see nor hear them, then slowly turned and walked back into the empty house.

Once they were gone, I wondered why they left so mysteriously that hot summer morning. Later that day, I learned that it was to haul watermelons to cities in the North. Times were hard, money was short, and neither of them had skills or education. Furthermore, Walter had no regular job. He made a marginal living by trading, hauling things and occasionally doing farm work when he could get it. Always full of hope to get rich, this trip was to be the first step in establishing his hoped-for produce hauling empire. Perhaps Mom's reason was easier to fathom. She loved this little man who offered so little, but who dreamed so grandly. With a good sense of humor, he was quick with a grin and freely broke into song. Mom was constantly amused, and her affection was undisguised. Besides, with nothing of her own but four kids at home, and a lot of busted promises, she hung tight to the prospect that life had to get better.

As they drove toward the fulfillment of their hope and dreams, little did I know that my life was changing forever and that nothing would ever be the same again. We would all live our lives separated one from the other, just as the island was separated from the mainland, yet joined together like the land bridge. From that point on I would be responsible for the affairs and events that were to shape and mold me. Standing in the bright sunlight, on the threshold of my destiny, I was unaware and poorly prepared for what lay ahead. The only thing that I knew for sure was that in less than a week I would be fifteen years old.

CHAPTER FIFTEEN

WAITING

By mid-morning I was growing anxious waiting for Uncle Leon. Periodically, I looked down the dirt ruts that connected the house with the rest of the world, and then wandered through the empty house that now seemed foreign and uninviting. I wondered how far Walter and Mom had traveled now? Where were they going? When would they be back? This secret adventure about which I knew nothing seemed strange. And why had my ride not come? The questions were confusing, and I had no answers.

I ambled out of the barbed-wire-fenced yard and walked among the relic citrus grove searching for a tree that might still have some fruit this late in the year.

The grove had once contained more than four hundred trees. Planted forty two years earlier, and severely neglected, over time most trees had died and those that remained were old and at the end of their bearing life. The trees had never been well suited to this site. Citrus trees grow best on deep, sandy soil. The island's heavy soil and shallow water table created insufficient root space, keeping the trees under constant stress. Insects and diseases had taken their toll. Left unattended, purple scale insects coated the twigs and were slowly sucking the life from any twig smaller than a pencil. Sooty Mold, a fungus common in neglected citrus trees covered the leaves with a black patina. Lichens covered their bark, and rotted limbs and twigs pointed skyward like bony fingers. Spider webs of Spanish moss hung from the limbs. The leaves, still wet with dew, soaked my clothes when I brushed against them. It seemed a miracle that the bedraggled survivors bore any fruit at all.

Finally, I found the tree that I had been looking for and picked one of the few remaining oranges. The skin was leathery but the flesh was sweet and juicy with small flecks of red in the pulp. The other trees had lost their fruit several weeks earlier, but this one tree still had a few hard to reach oranges. The trees were seedling varieties and many of the trees bore fruit that was unlike any other tree. It had been a family orchard, designed to provide fruit for home use and local market sales. It was important that the many varieties for home use ripened at different times throughout the season from October through April. The trees probably had been planted by Mr. Wilcox or Mr. Hansen, who lived there when my Grandfather Albert King was raising my mother and her siblings on the adjacent property on Cypress Island.

Down the road I suddenly saw a cattle truck cross the bridge and rumble along behind the row of wax myrtle. As it came into better view, I realized that it was not the one that I was looking for. The truck pulled up to the front gate and the island's caretaker, asked, "Walter and your Mamma home?" He always wanted to know if they were home when he arrived, but I knew that it was not Walter that he wanted to see. His interest in my mother was not well disguised. A crude man approximately fifty years old, he was never really welcome when he dropped in to check on things, but he was the care taker for the absentee owner of the property. Twenty or so yearlings were grazing the island that day and he was there to look after them.

"No," I replied, and shifted to one foot.

The caretaker squinted and looked me over. Tobacco juice had oozed from the corner of his mouth and slowly slid down his unshaven face. "Where they at?" he demanded.

"I don't know," I replied feeling more uncomfortable by the

minute.

"What you mean you don't know where they at?" His tone grew harsher. "They didn't just disappear in thin air did they?" He shifted his weight in the truck seat and began to stare intently at the boy in front of him. "When they coming back?"

"They didn't say."

He shook his head with growing disbelief. "Didn't say where they was going or when they was coming back? Who's gonna look after these cattle when I'm not around?"

Suddenly I could see the thread of his concern. He had rented the house to Mom to provide security for the cattle. The fact that she was an attractive 36 year old divorcee did not hurt her chances of renting the property at an affordable rate. Before Walter came to live with us, Mom told Aunt Betty that the caretaker had shown an interest in her but that she had discouraged him. He now only looked at Mom when he made his weekly visits to check the cattle.

Walter teased Mom about those long, drawn-out stares and the caretaker's frequent trips to the artesian well that brought a steady stream of cool, sweet water from deep within the earth. Like the rest of us, he would stand under the shade of the mango tree and pour water over his head after he drank his fill. Although he was often made fun of, the caretaker was never turned away from the well.

He continued to press me. "You going to stay here and look after these cows?"

"No, I'm going to Uncle Leon's house," I said. "He's coming for me later this morning."

"Damn!" He ran his fingers through the thin shock of greasy black hair, backed out of the drive and went to check on the cattle. When he later returned and began to question me again, I suggested that he talk with Aunt Ruth. He accepted my suggestion and left without further comment. It was obvious that he was deeply disappointed by what he felt was a failure by Mom to fulfill her commitment to stay on the island or, at least, to notify him of their departure.

I walked down by the barn. The few remaining chickens searched for grain where the milk cow had been fed that morning. They were game chickens, beautiful birds with orange and black feathers, half wild and never fat. They required little care and less feed. The eggs they laid were always well hidden, but when we could find them, were appreciated. In recent weeks the flock had been trimmed to eight hens and a rooster because neither Walter nor Mom were working. The birds were capable of finding their own food and would be fine until Mom returned. Next to the barn, the hog pen lay empty. Two weeks earlier we had eaten the last shoat.

Noon came and there was no sign of Uncle Leon. I found and ate two more oranges and a grapefruit that was so old that the seeds had sprouted. I checked the cupboard to see if Mom had overlooked anything. She hadn't.

I waited, but he did not come. By late afternoon the air was thick with humidity and dark clouds were forming thunder heads on the horizon. How stupid I had been! Uncle Leon was not coming! If so he would have been here by now! Did he forget? Or was I being left to fend for myself?

Suddenly the wind began to blow, and the air cooled. The sky turned dark and sheets of rain fell to the earth. Taking shelter on the back porch I pondered my predicament for an hour while the rain poured down from the heavens. I now realized that I could not resolve these questions by myself. By now it was after five o' clock, and the rain had slowed to a steady drizzle. I could no longer wait. I needed to do something. I picked up my sack of clothes and locked the house, and left the key under the well-stone. I started walking down the dirt ruts toward the bridge but had gone less than a hundred yards before Aunt Ruth's pickup truck appeared from behind the wax myrtles by the bridge.

Aunt Ruth was surprised to see me. "I thought that Uncle Leon was supposed to pick you up," she said while motioning me to get in out of the rain.

"He was."

Ruth frowned. "It's not like him to forget. Walter and your Mom told me that he would be here by noon to get you. You had anything to eat?"

"Nothing but oranges and a grapefruit since breakfast," I said.

Ruth was growing more upset by the minute but I was not sure who her anger was directed at. "I would have brought you something to eat if I had known. I can't believe that he forgot. Well I have to milk this cow now, and then I will take you to Uncle Leon's house."

At the sight of the truck, the milk cow came quickly to the barn. Ruth took a bucket of feed from the truck and carried it to the feeding trough. The cow settled into feeding and Ruth collected the milk in a white porcelain bucket. "Go to the house and get a glass and I will give you some milk. You must be hungry."

Two glasses later, we were on our way across the bridge to Ruth's house where she stopped to drop off the milk. She continued driving toward Kissimmee. Along the way I asked if she knew more about my mother's trip than I did. Ruth was dismayed. "I thought that you knew. They are going to sell watermelons. Walter said that they could earn enough money in three to four weeks of selling watermelons to live on all year long. I somehow doubt it, but that's what Walter said."

The wind shield wipers slapped time with the rattles made by the wooden sideboards on the truck as it traveled over the bricks that paved North Main Street. Huge live oaks lined the street and rain dropped gently from the sky, rolled over the green leaves, and slid down the Spanish moss onto the red brick road. The wet landscape made a kaleidoscope of misty color that seemed out of focus in the cloud- darkened light.

Aunt Ruth said, "We will go by Melvin's store. He might be there at this time of day." Uncle Leon went to the store almost every day to buy fresh groceries, pick up messages and make small talk with friends and acquaintances. Melvin's store served as a major center for coordinating cattle related business and ranchers could be seen there several times each week.

Arriving at the store, we quickly learned that Uncle Leon was not there. The word was that he had been building fence for a cattle operation out on Boggy Creek and they were not sure that he would be there by closing time at six o' clock.

Aunt Ruth decided to take me to Uncle Leon's house. She had left her older daughter Barbara in charge of Barbara's half siblings, Bruce and Cathy Sullivan, as well as my younger brother and sisters. It was now a quarter past six and Aunt Ruth needed to return as soon as possible to prepare the evening meal. Once again we started down Main Street.

Suddenly Uncle Leon's truck appeared, coming toward us. Ruth waved and both trucks stopped on opposite sides of the street. Ruth rolled down her window and yelled out "I have something for you". Quick as a flash, I grabbed my sack of clothes, thanked Aunt Ruth, hurried across the rain-slick road and climbed into the cab of the truck. At last I was where I was supposed to be and I was looking forward to supper.

CHAPTER SIXTEEN

THE ARRIVAL

Leon Allen looked down at the bedraggled kid with the rain-soaked paper bag who had just climbed into his truck. "Where the hell you going?" he demanded without being too harsh. For years I had bummed rides whenever I saw his old truck rumbling about town, therefore he was not surprised to see me. There was almost always a small sack of candy and peanuts in the glove department. He ate the peanuts, but the candy was for any kid he might run across in the course of his travels. Uncle Leon had never married but he liked children and a sack of goodies made sure that they liked him. His gruff greetings were always a mixture of inquiry and teasing. Nevertheless, I immediately was made uneasy by his question.

"I'm coming to live with you," I replied with my strongest voice.

"The hell you say."

"Mamma and Walter told me that you were coming to pick me up this morning, but I guess you forgot. But that's OK because Aunt Ruth said that she would bring me over." I was talking fast because Uncle Leon was looking more startled by the minute. I was definitely losing ground with each passing phrase.

"And who the hell told them that it was OK for you to live with me? Why the hell can't they take care of you?" Uncle Leon's eyes narrowed and the tone of his voice was more solemn than when I had first entered the truck.

The truck cab was filled with smoke from the King Edward

Cigar clinched tightly between his teeth. I looked down at my feet, then back at the man who awaited my answer as he drove toward Melvin Johnson's store.

"I don't know."

A man in his late fifties, his steel blue eyes were framed by his round, suntanned face. He was a man who shaved irregularly, and after two days of not shaving, his stubble of a beard perfectly matched the color of his thin gray hair. Leon Allen stood no taller than 5 feet, 9 inches but was a powerful man with a barrel chest and well muscled arms. He wore clothing that distinguished him as a working-class cattleman: Levi jeans, a plaid, cotton, short-sleeved shirt, wide leather belt, western boots that showed their age and a ten-gallon felt hat. He had worked all of his life in the cattle trade and had the scars to show for it. His skin was weathered from years of hard outdoor living and his hands were calloused from years of manual labor. Crows-feet wrinkles outlined his eyes and there were lines forming at the corners of his mouth. Excessive drinking as a young man had led to the onset of diabetes and he was slow to heal when cut. His bare arms bore the scars from many years of fence building and there were new wounds from six days of working with barbed wire under a sub-tropical sun. The June heat and dirt from digging post holes made healing even more difficult. Building fences in a cattle community like Kissimmee provided a steady income because he was recognized as the best in his trade.

The plaid shirt he wore was wet with sweat, as were his denim jeans. When he turned to speak to me his shirt stuck to the back of the leather seat. Even with the truck's cab filled with smoke, he had the smell of sweat that comes from hard work. Leon Allen was a man who enjoyed cigars when he relaxed, but preferred Apple Chewing Tobacco when he was working at a job where he needed to keep his hands free. Building fences was just such a job and tobacco juice stained the corner of his mouth. He was the quintessential image of a man returning from a day of ranch work but instead of his day getting better at quitting time, his was rapidly turning sour.

Leon Vernon Allen -"Uncle Leon"

"Walter and Mama went up North to sell watermelons. They said that I was supposed to stay with you and Walter said that it was all set up." I was giving it my best shot but still not making much progress.

"Well, they damn sure didn't tell me anything about it. Selling watermelons! What the hell has got into Walter! Your Mamma must have lost her damn mind when she took up with him. They actually told you that I was going to pick you up? When and where the hell was I supposed to do all of this?"

Uncle Leon's questions were coming too fast for me to answer and his face was growing redder with every new inquiry. Then, as if at a loss for what else to say, he began a long well-practiced monologue of cursing the likes of which I had never heard before. In the years ahead I learned that it was a mantra he used mostly in his not too infrequent rages at the state of affairs in the Allen family. But now I sat stunned and silent on the farthest most part of the cracked leather seat, making myself as small as possible. Sensing my withdrawal and realizing that I was not responsible for the problem at hand, he asked, "When did you last eat?"

"Breakfast," I replied in a voice much more subdued than when I earlier had spoken.

Uncle Leon continued cursing until we got to the dirt parking lot behind Melvin's store.

"There's peanuts in the glove box. I will be back in a few minutes. Then we will get some supper." The store had closed but Melvin was still there and the back door was unlocked. Uncle Leon walked in and picked out a quart of milk, meat, bread, bananas and an assortment of canned goods. He returned to the truck just as I finished the last of the peanuts.

The trip to Uncle Leon's house lasted about fifteen minutes but seemed much longer as he ranted about the shortcomings of the family in general, and this situation in particular. When we arrived, I was glad to get out of the truck and move around. Once inside, I greeted my brother Leon who had lived with Uncle Leon since he left home at age eleven. He was surprised to see me but waited until we were alone later that evening to get the details of my arrival. My brother had long ago learned not to ask questions when our uncle was upset. In the kitchen, Uncle Leon fried the beef steak that he had brought from the store, warmed a pot of leftover mixed vegetables and meat scraps, opened two cans of turnip greens and boiled a pot of grits. Boiled strong chicory-flavored coffee, milk and whole wheat bread rounded out the meal.

The three of us ate by the light of a kerosene lamp, with the only sounds being an occasional request to pass something. I ate almost everything that he had prepared, and then drank all of the remaining milk. By the time we had finished the meal, Uncle Leon was beginning to calm down. He asked me once again when Walter and my mother were coming back, and I again told him that I thought that they were due in three weeks to a month, but I could not be sure. Hearing my answer again, he shook his head, slowly stood up, lit a new cigar, then walked to the back porch. He sat alone on the porch steps in the night air feeding slices of bread to his horse, Fanny, while my brother and I washed and dried the dishes.

After we finished the dishes, we each took turns bathing on the back porch using water drawn from fifty-five gallon steel drums that were strategically placed to catch water from the tin roof. Those barrels were the only source of water for bathing, washing dishes, and watering the horse. Care was taken to waste as little water as possible. Over the years there had been a number of deep wells drilled on the property, but the fine sand had clogged the point and the wells failed. Drinking water, taken from the flowing well at the slaughterhouse, was hauled weekly to his house in five-gallon and one-gallon jugs.

Uncle Leon showed me a cot in the saddle room and gave me sheets and a pillow. The room was approximately 8 by 12 feet and was used to store saddles, bridles, saddle blankets, two shot guns and other miscellaneous farm and household items. One of the guns was ancient and had not been fired in the last thirty years. A ten gauge, it had been handed down to Uncle Leon from his father when he died. The gun was the sum total of his inheritance. The other gun was an old double-barreled, twelve gauge in good working order. For years it had been Uncle Leon's main shot gun but as he had become more affluent, he had added newer and better guns. A 22 caliber rifle was kept by the back door and a relatively new, twelve gauge stood in the corner of his bedroom next to his bed. The guns were always loaded, and each was strategically located. He had grown up in the swamps and palmetto prairies of Florida during the turbulent first twenty years of the century when cracker families relied first upon themselves for protection, then upon the law.

My brother Leon slept in the bedroom adjacent to the saddle room. The room contained a standard cast iron, double bed that sagged with age. It was the bed that Uncle Leon's mother, Nancy, had slept in before her death in 1940. The room also had a chest of drawers, a closet for hanging clothes and a steamer trunk at the foot of the bed for storing blankets and other bedding materials.

About 8 o'clock, Uncle Leon retired to his room to read a paperback novel as was his custom. He had not passed beyond the third year in school, but he read well and his novels transported him to other places and times. Seldom did an evening pass that he did not read for at least an hour. Western and detective novels were his favorites. He would lie in bed and read quietly by the light of his kerosene lamp.

The glass kerosene lamp by his bed had to be pumped like a lantern and it operated using ash mantles instead of a wick. It was almost as bright as an electric light and was the only truly adequate light in the house. It was never moved from his bedside table. The three remaining lamps were traditional wick lamps that produced almost as much soot in their glass chimneys as yellow-hued light.

One lamp was always kept in the kitchen; the other two were moved freely around the house. My brother always took one of them to his room at the end of the day, but there was no place to set a lamp down in the saddle room. Later that evening I left my lamp on the dining room table, as instructed, and it provided enough light to prepare for bed.

Once Uncle Leon was in bed, my brother and I retreated to the back porch where in low voices he asked questions and I filled him in on the day's events. He, in turn, advised me on the things that I needed to know while I was living at their house. Get up early, find chores that need doing, don't track sand into the house, pick up the eggs and feed the chickens were on his list. He finished by telling me "Never drink all of the milk." He always made sure to leave about three inches of milk in the carton. With no refrigeration the milk would turn to clabber overnight and Uncle Leon enjoyed it with his morning breakfast. I took note and never again drank all of the milk at supper time.

He and Uncle Leon had been aware that our family had been struggling for some time, but their intense, mutual dislike for Walter had made it difficult for Uncle Leon to provide the support that we needed.

Before Walter became a part of Mom's life, Uncle Leon served as an economic safety net for my mother just as he had done for so many others.

In fact, for most of his life, Uncle Leon had cared for others. He and his mother had taken in Dad and his two brothers when Will and Ruby had divorced. Then he took care of his mother for the remainder of her years and nursed her through her final days. Now he was providing financial support for my grandfather who was his older brother.

When we finished talking, my brother and I said good night to one another and to Uncle Leon before retiring to our rooms. It had been a most remarkable day! For the first time in six years, Leon and I were living under the same roof. My stomach was full, and suddenly, I was in the care of the most stable member of the Allen clan.

Even with all of this I could not quit replaying the events of the day. I had been left with no food and with no certainty that I had a place to go to. It was an old song that had been played many times in my brief life. I had been shuffled on short notice between my parents, or left with relatives, and on one occasion, with strangers. For the first time in the last several years, I had the overwhelming feeling that things had turned out fine.

As I lay on the cot in the little room that was to be my home for the foreseeable future, I smelled the leather from the saddles and felt the heavy night air come drifting in the window and wash over me. I was happy to be reunited with my brother. As I lay there, I remembered the stories Grandpa Will and Uncle Leon had told of two young cowboys punching cattle north of the Everglades. Visions of their stories danced wildly in my head and I imagined that it was me and my brother, not Uncle Leon and Grandpa Will, who had brought the cattle through the great hurricane of 1926. It was Leon and I who had killed the rattle snakes, branded the calves, and rescued the cattle when they became mired in a bog. And it was us who lived in the line shacks to make sure the cattle were not rustled in the days before every square acre of Florida was fenced and posted. The sudden sense of well-being was overwhelming. I drifted between fantasy and reality until sleep finally overcame me.

With my last conscious thought, I vowed that I would never again allow myself to be so dependent that I could be left again. My life was now in my hands; I had to make it work out the best I could.

PART TWO

FINDING A PATH THROUGH THE BRIAR THICKET

CHAPTER SEVENTEEN

BUILDING FENCES

When I woke up the next morning, Uncle Leon and my brother were already up and dressed. Uncle Leon was frying eggs and boiling a pot of coffee. Remembering what my brother had told me the night before, I hurried to put on my jeans, and get my face washed in the basin on the back porch. Uncle Leon was in a much better mood and greeted me with a mild reproach. "Well boy, you slept so damn long your head's done got hairy." I grinned at the thought but said nothing. It was good to see him in a good mood.

After we had eaten, my brother headed out to work at Dr. Ed Whaley's Veterinary Clinic. He had been working at the clinic and on his ranch for the last few years. On this day, he would be working inside helping Dr. Whaley and his assistant Albert treat dogs and cats.

Uncle Leon announced that he would be at Dr. Whaley's ranch to continue building fence and asked if I wanted to go with him or stay home. "I want to go with you," I replied.

"Well, you will be working all day, and it's going to be a hot one."

"I want to go."

"Well, get in the truck."

Unwilling to be left behind, I scrambled out to the truck.

Uncle Leon looked at my shoes, then the jeans and tee shirt that I was wearing and said, "Before I take you to work, we better get you some work boots." He drove to the Army Surplus Store across from Whaley's Veterinary Clinic on North Main

Street. The store sold a variety of Army surplus goods as well as work clothes. He chose for me a pair of heavy ankle-high lace-up leather work boots. They had a hard toe and a thick sole strong enough to protect your feet in the harshest environment. It was the first pair of boots that I ever had. When he finished selecting boots, he added socks, two pair of new jeans, a leather belt and three plaid short-sleeved cotton shirts like those that he wore. I could not remember when I got so many clothes at one time. It felt like Christmas.

From there we went to the work site on Boggy Creek Road. Bill Tyson was waiting on us and surprised that we were so late. He had started digging postholes at eight and it was now almost nine o' clock.

"Preacher, who's that you got with you," he inquired. "Preacher" was one of two nicknames given to Uncle Leon by his men friends because of his salty language. Although given to such language around men, he was always respectful, and somewhat shy, when in the presence of women.

"Eunice's boy. He's staying with me for a spell. I wasn't looking for him but now I got him AND his brother."

"You were so late I was getting worried about you. Afraid you might of had a heart attack."

Uncle Leon shrugged his shoulders and said, "No such luck." They both laughed.

Uncle Leon handed me a pair of well-worn leather gloves and told me that my job was going to be putting posts in the holes that the two men were digging.

Bill Tyson and Uncle Leon were friends and partners in fence building and in the weekly slaughter of cattle. They worked well together. Each man knew what needed to be done and did it without consent of the other. Even so, there was never any doubt who was in charge.

Uncle Leon's other nickname was "Major". It was a name that he sometimes bristled at, but never commented on. Few men called him that to his face. Nevertheless, it was a name that suited him. He was so well-respected by those who knew him that he was always in charge if he was on a worksite. Dr. Whaley loved to tell the story about when Uncle Leon had built the cow pens on Whaley's ranch. In the years ahead I heard him recount it several times while laughing and telling the story. The pens were on the same large property that we now were building fence on. Dr. Whaley said that when Uncle Leon had finished constructing the cow pens, he realized that it would be necessary to have a tack shed for storing saddles, bridles, vet medicines, barbed wire and small tools. He also wanted an open-air shed to store hay, and to house the big John Deere Model R diesel tractor that was used for farm chores. Uncle Leon asked Dr. Whaley a few questions and then assured him that he would have it marked out with stakes the next day.

When Dr. Whaley returned to the work site, he said that he told Uncle Leon that what he had marked out was too small and in the wrong place. Uncle Leon's answer was "Ed, who the hell's building this, you or me?" With a cackle Dr. Whaley would say, "I got back in my car and went back to town. When it was finished the shed was the right size and it was in the right place."

To make a straight fence line, the men first planted large pull-posts at the corners of the property. If the fence line was longer than the wire on a bale of barbed wire, pull-posts were erected at an appropriate distance from the starting position. Once the wire was stapled to the starting post, a one inch diameter metal pipe about four feet long was inserted through the center of the bale. The bale of wire was then unrolled by two people who walked parallel to one another, toward the second pull post. Both people unrolling the bale had to be careful so that the bale did not slide to either side and cut the hand of his partner. Stiff leather gloves were essential. After a short trial, I became Bill Tyson's partner in this task.

Once the wire reached the pull post, wire stretchers were

used to tighten the wire. Uncle Leon then walked the length of the wire, using a claw hammer to free the wire from any brush or other obstacles that might interfere with the wire being made taut. He used the claws of the hammer to move the wire instead of his hands in case the wire broke under the strain of the stretchers. This was the most dangerous phase of fence building. If a wire under tension broke, the barbs would cut like a saw as it recoiled. After the wire was pulled straight, and under the proper tension, it was time to dig fence-post holes. Fence-post holes were dug along the path of the wire. The two men were seasoned fence builders and they kept a steady rhythm of digging holes, sometimes talking, sometimes quiet. I placed the posts in the holes, snugged them up to the wire and kicked the sand into the hole with the side of my new boots. A shovel handle was used to tamp down the soil and firm up the post in a vertical position.

By ten o' clock, the temperature had reached the low nineties and the humidity was approaching similar numbers. Our clothing was soaked with sweat, that ran down our faces and dripped off our chins. The men periodically wiped their faces with handkerchiefs that were already wet. They did not talk now about anything but the weather.

"Drink plenty of water, Bill. I don't want you to get a heat stroke. Take a rest if you need to," Bill Tyson admonished me.

I kept working until they took a break. We rested in the shade of the truck bed and drank our fill of water from the gallon jug. The jug was getting low by now, and the men discussed whether one of them should go to the wind mill and fill the jug. They decided to wait until lunch time.

"It's a hell of a lot hotter than yesterday," chimed in Uncle Leon. "And it's supposed to be even hotter this afternoon."

After resting a few minutes, the work resumed. The sound of the post hole diggers penetrating the sandy soil was now broken only by the thud of the diggers hitting the hardpan. Hardpan is a layer of compacted, dense soil beneath the surface of the top soil. It varies in its depth from the surface based upon the soil profile. Uncle Leon and Bill Tyson were hitting hardpan six inches short of the depth needed to make the posts stable. They toiled on in the heat.

At noon the work stopped. We went back home for lunch, and to take a break from the heat and humidity. I did not know it at the time but that was unusual. Uncle Leon usually brought a wooden box of camp cooking supplies and prepared a meal at the work site. Canned pork and beans, whole wheat bread, boiled coffee, and sirloin steaks that he had picked up from Melvin's store before work were standard fare. Beans were warmed in a frying pan and coffee was boiled over a wood fire. The steaks were supported on forked sticks that he cut from a nearby bush, and placed close to the fire's edge. When one side of the meat was seared he reversed the meat and cooked the other side. This day was too hot for cooking.

When we got back to the house Uncle Leon and Bill Tyson began preparing a meal. I sat down on the old leather couch in the living room, leaned back and passed out from exhaustion and dehydration.

I woke up with Bill Tyson shaking my shoulder. "Time to eat. You need to drink some water."

After lunch, we all rested for an hour before returning to work. Uncle Leon suggested that I stay home because of the heat. I told him that I wanted to go back with him and Bill.

"All right, if you think that you can handle it. But drink more water this afternoon." He handed me one of his old, sweat-stained ten-gallon hats and said "Put this on your head. It will help." A skinny, white-haired kid with a hat like that must have been a comical sight.

I finished that long hot day in June, 1954, alongside two seasoned working adults. I was not their equal in physical labor, or in the knowledge of what needed to be done, but I had held my own and they liked my grit. Both men had treated me like an adult and that was something that I had always yearned for. Now that I had their respect, I was determined to carry my share of the load whenever possible. My first day with Uncle Leon had been a good one.

CHAPTER EIGHTEEN

THE CATTLE MARKET

Two days later we finished the fence. The weather had cooled some and was now into the high eighties but the needle on the humidity had not moved much. I was glad that we were done with fencing for a while.

Wednesday was sale day at the cattle market. Almost every week Uncle Leon hauled someone's cattle to be sold, and my first week was no different. Rising early, we made our way to an elderly man's house to pick up five steers that he had penned the night before. Uncle Leon and the man talked briefly before we loaded the cattle into Uncle Leon's truck.

We arrived at the market about 7:30 a.m. and waited in line with others who were bringing cattle for sale. The man in charge assigned a number to our load, and Uncle Leon told him the name of the cattle's owner. The cattle were sold later that day at auction. On this day Uncle Leon had only a single load of cattle, but he sometimes had more than one.

The auction started after lunch. The cattle to be sold were brought into an arena and automatically weighed. Sometimes they were sold as individuals and at other times, they were sold in lots of three or four at a time. Buyers sat on wooden seats in the semicircular stands across from the auctioneer. As soon as the cattle were in the arena, the auctioneer began his monotonous chant while surveying the crowd. Buyers bid with nods of the head or the twitch of a hand. The auctioneer and the buyers for big slaughterhouses such as Lykes Brothers near Tampa staged a 45 second ballet of buying and selling, before the cattle were whisked out of the arena to be hauled away. Large numbers of cattle were sold each week, and the sale often continued into the evening hours.

The market was a weekly meeting place for those who made their living from cattle. It served as a social gathering place and a place to make business contacts. It also served a great hamburger in the cafe. Uncle Leon usually left after dropping off his load but returned when the sale started. It was a good place to pick up work hauling cows or building fence. Melvin Johnson was always there to buy four steers for his meat market. I was amazed that out of the chaotic atmosphere of the auction, orderly business was being conducted. Everyone knew the drill.

On Thursday morning we again got up early and went to the market to pick up Melvin's steers. The office said that another person had bought a steer and wanted it slaughtered, so we loaded five steers in the truck. We took them to the slaughterhouse at Melvin's ranch on Shingle Creek. Bill Tyson was waiting on us. He had opened up the facility and made it ready for the day's work.

The building was perfectly engineered for its purpose. After the steers were unloaded into a holding pen, two steers at a time were driven back up the loading chute, as if to be loaded into the truck. It was a trap; doors were closed in front of and behind them. One side of the slaughterhouse was part of the loading chute. With the admonition, "Goodbye you son-of-a-bitch," and a single 22 caliber bullet to their brain, the animals were dead. They did not suffer. The part of the slaughterhouse wall that made up one side of the loading chute had a large overhead door that could be raised manually to allow us to winch the dead cattle onto the slaughterhouse floor. The hooks on the electric winch were inserted into the hind ankles of the carcass between the bone and tendon. The carcass could then be raised as needed to process the animal. Uncle Leon and Bill Tyson made quick work of bleeding, skinning, gutting and quartering each animal.

Each quarter of the steer's carcass was hung in the truck on meat hooks attached to two by six inch timbers and covered with a tarp for their trip back to Melvin's refrigerated locker room. Melvin then processed the carcass for sale in his store. The fifth steer was cut up and packaged by Melvin for the person who wanted to fill their freezer.

The floor of the slaughterhouse was made of smooth finished concrete that sloped to a central channel. The channel allowed blood and clean-up water to be carried to an underground septic system. The house and the septic system were connected by a tin pipe that could be easily removed. Uncle Leon always removed the pipe and placed a wash tub under the spout to catch the blood. When it was time to clean the house, the tub was removed, the pipe replaced, and the slaughterhouse thoroughly cleaned.

At the end of the day, on our way home, Uncle Leon dropped off the blood to Jake and Annie, an old black couple that raised hogs. They had known each other for years. Jake now was too old to work but his hogs provided income to supplement his garden and chickens. Jake mixed the blood with grain meal and then cooked the mixture in a cast-iron wash pot to feed his hogs. He was always happy to see us arrive. They would always talk a little about how things were going. Annie wanted to know all about this new boy with Uncle Leon. I don't think that Jake and Annie had much company.

When we finally got back to the house it was time to store the hides of the freshly-slaughtered steers. Uncle Leon charged a penny a pound live weight to butcher an animal and he kept the hide. Hides were salted for storage, and once a year a hide dealer came by and bought them for making leather. To keep the hides from rotting we first spread them out on the ground with the hair side down. Rock salt was liberally applied to the fleshy side and then the hide was rolled up, making sure that the newly salted side was not exposed. The hides were then placed in steel fifty five-gallon drums and covered with a piece of corrugated tin and a cinder block to keep out rain water. Each hide was worth three to four dollars.

By the end of that first Wednesday and Thursday I was beginning to have a full appreciation of how hard Uncle Leon worked every day. I lived in Kissimmee, known as the Cow Capital of Florida, and yet knew very little about the trade. Uncle Leon was teaching me, but there was a lot yet to learn.

There was a break in the work schedule the following week. We went to Melvin's store every day and Uncle Leon visited with Melvin, his sister Carmy, and an assortment of friends and clients for perhaps an hour. They were all good friends and had no problem mixing work and pleasure.

Early that week, when we left the store, Uncle Leon drove to Dr. Whaley's office to pick up a check for the fence that was now completed. My brother was there working in the clinic. He was planning to become a veterinarian once he finished college, and it was clear that Dr. Whaley was holding a position for him. Leon was fortunate to be given this opportunity. He still worked on the ranch but was logging more and more time at the clinic.

The two men spoke for a few minutes and then Uncle Leon received his check and one for Bill Tyson from the bookkeeper.

As we started out the door Dr. Whaley said, "Wait a minute Leon. If you are not using that boy this week, I could use some help sprucing up the outside of this place."

Uncle Leon replied "I don't need him. What do you want him to do?"

"The flower beds have gone to pot and look awful. I'll have him clean out the weeds and Bermuda grass, and then fertilize and mulch the plants. It'll keep him busy for a couple of days."

I jumped at the chance being offered and reported for work the next morning. It was hands and knees work, pulling weeds and digging out the Bermuda grass underground runners. Dr. Whaley had a sack of fertilizer and a load of mulch delivered, and when I finished two days later, he came out for an inspection. He approved of my work and asked me to work on the extensive flower beds at his home at the lake. My brother Leon provided transportation with Dr. Whaley's Willys Jeep truck, letting me drive to get familiar with traffic. I worked an additional four days at their home, When I finished, Mrs. Whaley was pleased and so was I. Little did I know that I was auditioning for my brother's job. Leon would leave to attend the University of Florida in September, and Dr. Whaley was looking for his replacement.

CHAPTER NINETEEN

SALVATION

Now that I had worked part-time for Dr. Whaley, Bill Tyson decided that he had a few days of work for me. Bill owned a ten-acre orange grove and a small herd of beef cows that supplied most of his income. The work with Uncle Leon was supplemental.

In his late fifties, Bill was not currently married, although I believe that he had been earlier in life. A man of medium build, a modest pot belly and thinning hair, he smiled easily, and often kidded me when I was around him. He made an attempt to make a teen-age boy feel comfortable in his presence.

Several days after I finished Mrs. Whaley's landscape work, Bill picked me up one morning and drove me to his home. A part of the ten-acre grove needed hoeing to keep the weeds from going to seed. Bill had hoed more than forty percent of the trees, but had grown tired of the labor in the hot, sticky weather. I was glad to get the work. The mature trees shaded the ground, so the weeds were sparse under the trees and the light sand made hoeing young weeds easy. Each tree only took a few minutes. Most of the work was in the shade except at mid-day when the sun penetrated the alleys between the trees. The humidity was uncomfortably high.

At noon, Bill prepared a hot lunch and told me to pick some limes. He made limeade for the two of us and then poured a generous portion of vodka in his, even though he had diabetes. After lunch, we sat for an hour in rocking chairs on his back porch and he expounded on a wide variety of stories and opinions. I think that he liked having a boy to talk to.

On the third day, I finished the grove. Bill inspected my work, paid me and brought me home. With the money I had made, I bought a few more clothes and a regular pair of shoes. I had been wearing the work boots every day since I had arrived at Uncle Leon's house. I now had a little spending money.

It was now time to plant pasture grass on Dr. Whaley's ranch. That summer we planted pangola grass. The grass is native of the South American subtropics. It grows fast and can reach a height of three feet. It is an excellent grass for making hay but is easily over grazed.

My brother Leon was now in charge of preparing the ground for planting. The previous summer, he and I had picked up stumps on a large field in preparation for planting watermelons. Dr. Whaley had rented the newly-cleared land to a watermelon grower. The crop was timed to meet the early May, northern market. The melons had been picked and shipped by June first, and my brother had leveled the twelve-foot rows to the land's original contour, using the John Deere tractor and a disc.

Dr. Whaley rented a grass planter and Leon hired three older boys and me to help him. The planter was a home-made machine that would never have passed current OSHA standards. It consisted of a two-wheeled, wooden trailer bed, with four metal planters, individually attached to the back of the trailer. It was pulled behind the tractor.

The day began by filling the trailer bed with fresh-cut stems of pangola grass. Each of the four boys that were planting sat on metal seats, facing backwards, on their individual metal planters. There were no seat belts. Our feet rested in metal stirrups on either side of a large metal disc that was notched so that the long stems of pangola grass could be inserted in the notch, and pulled into the soil. Two metal wheels, set at angles behind the disc, closed the notch in the soil around the newly-planted grass stems. Each metal planter rose and fell with the terrain making the ride rough and unpredictable. Leon drove the tractor slow to provide as much safety and comfort as possible. No one was injured but it was a dangerous machine.

The work was finished shortly before mid-July 1954. I had now been living with Uncle Leon for more than four weeks. When my brother and I returned on the final day of grass planting, Uncle Leon was already home and waiting for us. He greeted me with the news "Your mammy's back." He was ready for me to return home to Aultman Island, but I had grown to like my new life.

At first I froze, then screwed up all the courage that I could muster and said, "I would like to live here with you." He was caught off guard and stood there looking at me for a good three minutes while thinking over what I had just requested. He, no doubt, was conflicted. My brother, Leon, was leaving for college in the fall, and he would have no more responsibility to anyone other than those he chose to help. He also had not talked with Mom. Walter and Mom had been home a few days and had retrieved my siblings, but had made no effort to inquire about me. They never did.

Finally he spoke. "Well boy, if you stay here, you may never get so you like it, but you will God-damned sure know what work is!" By now, he knew that I would work, but he could not know whether I liked it. My heart began racing. I had gambled and won.

With Uncle Leon's short declaration, my life had taken a giant step forward.

I now had gained the things that I wanted most in life: stability, security, acceptance and respect. Given her circumstances, Mom had done the best that she could to provide stability and security. She could not do it alone. I had wanted Dad's acceptance, but I had failed in that endeavor and in disgust, he had sent me to live with my grandfather. Finally, through hard work, I had earned the acceptance and respect of the most important man in the entire Allen clan. I was home safe. Salvation was at hand!

Over the next two months, I settled in at Uncle Leon's house for good, and took on more responsibility for house work and feeding Uncle Leon's horse and the dogs and chickens. Finding the eggs was a time consuming job that my brother now delegated to me.

Leon was transitioning out of the household and I was taking over all of his responsibilities. He took me to work with him every time he worked on the ranch and taught me how to service and drive the John Deere tractor. I could drive the tractor on the farm, but still could not drive an automobile unsupervised on the road, because at fifteen, I only had a learner's permit. Leon took it upon himself to let me drive the Willys Jeep truck as much as possible to improve my driving skills. By now I knew how to repair fence and perform a number of ranch tasks. My brother was preparing me to take his place when he left in September. Uncle Leon was teaching me ranch skills, and I was learning by doing.

Dr. Whaley's cows and one bull were Brahma, and another four of his five bulls were Black Angus. The Black Angus bulls fought every time a cow was in season, making fence repair a skill constantly needed. The Brahma bull did not fight much on such occasions and a disproportionate number of the calves were white, not black. This concerned Dr. Whaley because the Angus-Brahma cross calves were worth more money when sold at the market.

Later that summer, we cut, sun-cured, and baled into hay the pangola grass from another pasture and then stacked the rectangular bales of hay in the shed. It would not be needed until the next winter, when the pangola grass pasture was fenced off from the cattle to protect it from overgrazing, and the Pensacola Bahia grass was in short supply.

Before my brother left in September, I spent the week

shadowing him at the clinic. I started helping out after school and on Saturdays. When I first started in the clinic, Dr. Whaley showed me how to hold an animal in transit to and from the examining room, and on the examining table. With a grin and a chuckle, he also explained that my most important job was to make sure that he did not get bitten!

While that responsibility was paramount, most of my duties were designed to help his assistant, Albert, in the many daily responsibilities that fell to him. Albert was a black man in his forties who had been working at the clinic for many years. He and Dr. Whaley were a smooth-running team. I was assigned duties by both men, which was unusual in the segregated south.

Albert and I cleaned cages, fed animals, held patients and after each examination we washed and sterilized syringes and surgical instruments, as well as the white porcelain examining table. When pets were euthanized or died from natural causes, I buried them in the small field behind the clinic.

I quickly came to understand Dr. Whaley's deep respect for Albert. He was very professional. Albert and I talked a lot. He told me that he had played two years of football for the legendary Jake Gaither at Florida A&M University. He did not graduate but was well educated in a number of areas. When we worked until after dark, he often drove me home. It saved me a nearly three mile walk on unlit, sand roads. I returned the favor by giving him eggs for his family.

On Sunday mornings I went in early and fed the animals that were being held overnight and cleaned their cages. At ten o' clock, Dr. Whaley dropped by to care for each of his patients. There often were people waiting with dogs that had been bitten by snakes or were covered with ticks. Both cases were usually the result of Saturday night hunting trips. Those dogs were attended to first.

Snake-bitten dogs usually had swollen heads because that was where the snake stuck them. Dr. Whaley would lance the flesh at the fang marks and use rubber suction cup to draw out the venom and poisoned blood. I was always surprised to later learn that most of the dogs that he treated survived.

Dogs with a large number of ticks were dipped in a bath of an insecticidal solution. My arms also were exposed at the same time that I lowered the patient into the solution, and poured it over their head and backs. I vigorously washed my arms after each dipping to remove pesticide residue. I never knew what was in the dip and I never exhibited any side effects. I now suspect that it was DDT or Methoxychlor, both of which were low toxicity, chlorinated hydrocarbons that were later banned from use.

CHAPTER TWENTY

THE FALL CATTLE ROUNDUP

After school had started in the fall of 1954, I was involved in my first roundup. While it was a work day, it was also a social experience. Several cowboys and some of their family members were involved. It was always held on a Sunday to accommodate people's schedules and lasted until mid-afternoon. There usually were several riders and a dozen specially-trained dogs to work the cattle. Dogs were more effective than cowboys when cattle were in heavy brush or near swamps. Because many cattlemen pastured their cattle on unimproved pasture, dogs were essential for keeping the cattle in a circle until the riders could catch up. If the cattle evaded the dogs and made it into a swamp with water, it was very difficult to round them up.

Everyone had a special job each time we got together. I had no horse and therefore could not be a rider. Leon had sold his horse, Pal, before I came to live with Uncle Leon. He needed the money for tuition and other college expenses. My job that first year was to go with Uncle Leon to open the veterinary clinic and pick up the medicines that would be used that day. After I turned sixteen, I was able to drive myself to the clinic. Dr. Whaley had given me a key to the clinic so that I could let myself in on Sunday mornings to clean the cages and help care for the animals. On the Sundays that we worked cattle, I was excused and Albert opened early. My brother Leon had been given the same access for the past few years. I made an inventory of the medicines that we took and left it in the office.

Gallon jugs of a cobalt mixture would be needed to help the cattle better digest the grass that they ate. Phenothiazine, also in gallon jugs, would be needed to worm adult cattle, and a medicine called White Smear was to prevent or treat screwworms that infested fresh wounds.

When the riders and dogs left to find the cattle, my work began. I gathered wood for the branding fire and then oiled all of the hinges on the cow pen gates, making sure that they were in good working order. Next, I checked the boards on the pens to make sure that they were secure and that nails had not popped out since the last time these pens had been used.

When the dogs finally reached the cattle, they circled them until the riders arrived. The cattle were not moved immediately. With dogs on the perimeter, the calves clung to the mothers for protection. It was common for more than one person to have cattle in the herd. I suspected that was to make sure that everyone showed up to help. Now surrounded by dogs and cowboys, someone would take notice of which calf belonged to each cow. This was important when the calf was later branded. That person was referred to as the "Mammier."

The cattle were then driven back to the cow pens and separated into groups to be branded, marked, emasculated, wormed, and treated for nutritional deficiencies and/or screw worms. The animals in the holding pen were sent one at a time down a long, narrow, wooden path to a head chute. Searching for a path to freedom, the animals would stick their heads through the head chute and heavy timbers on each side would be closed around their neck. The cow could breath but could not go forward or backward.

One side of the chute was a gate that opened and a man would push an animal against the stationary side to bring it under control. Calves would be branded, and if it was a bull calf it was also emasculated. Melvin Johnson did the branding. Bill Tyson did the emasculation. The ears of calves were also marked as a means to identify the owner. Every animal had both a brand and a marked ear. Pieces of the ear were cut out in a pattern that was readily recognizable. Uncle Leon did the marking of animals and applied White Smear to the wounds. Our brand was O bar, with the bar beneath the O. The ear mark was read from left to right when the animal was facing you. Our mark was crop, two split, under bit, under bit, swallow fork. It was an old practice that later gave way to the more modern and humane method of using metal or plastic ear tags.

It was my job to put nose tongs tied to a rope in every animal's nose when it came into the head chute. I pulled their head up using the rope, slung over a wooden arm of the chute, to stabilize the animal. I was selected for this duty because most of the cows had horns and I had long arms. I also was more nimble than the adults and perhaps more expendable. I was never injured.

The brood cows were given six ounces of both cobalt and Phenothiazine and released. The entire procedure was usually completed in four minutes or less.

Wives would start showing up about eleven thirty with food and soon we were all sitting in the shade, talking, laughing and eating lunch. At the end of the day the cattle were released, and the riders took their horses and dogs and went home. I put out the branding fire, closed the cow pen gates and Uncle Leon and I took the unused medicines back to the clinic. The next time we did this it would be at someone else's property. Over the next three years there would be several such days. With each new roundup, I was gaining confidence and was becoming ever more accepted as a part of the working group.

Although the work was hard and I received no pay, I never got tired of doing it. I was passing into adulthood and enjoying the ride.

CHAPTER TWENTY-ONE

WORKING AND LEARNING AT THE CLINIC

School and work dominated my time in the tenth grade. Without an unrestricted driver's license I could only work at the clinic and at the Whaley's home. With Leon at the university, Dr. Whaley checked the cattle at his ranch and took me to open gates and scatter hay bales when pasture rations were short. The after-school work was part-time that first year. I could never depend on it, but I was employed about fifty percent of the afternoons. Each day that I worked, Dr. Whaley let me know whether or not to report the next day. My Saturday and Sunday morning work was dependable and I could plan accordingly.

Back at the clinic, Dr. Whaley began letting me watch him perform surgery when there was free time. The first time that I watched him and Albert cut open a cat I got a little light headed and he sent me out to get some fresh air. I was embarrassed, but soon recovered and returned to the operating room. He assured me that it was often the case when someone was new; it was the smell more than the sight. Over time, the operations no longer bothered me and I sometimes got to assist.

Albert usually assisted Dr. Whaley with surgery and he anticipated his every need. When I got the chance to help, Albert stood next to me in case he was needed. Dr. Whaley administered the anesthetic and performed the procedure; I handed him the instruments and medicines as he requested them. As he went about his work, Dr. Whaley talked constantly, teaching me the biology of the patient. While I had cleaned a lot of fish, chickens, and rabbits, and assisted with the slaughter of cattle, seeing the internal organs of a live animal and listening to his narration was fascinating. He was the best science teacher that I had that year.

His mentoring and biology lessons had convinced my brother, Leon, to choose the pre-vet, animal science major at the University of Florida. Now I was entertaining the same course of action. That thought did not last. The next year, when I turned sixteen and could drive to the ranch, it was obvious to both Dr. Whaley and me that I preferred working outdoors. I had grown tired of dealing with, and being bitten and scratched by, feisty little pets. I still found the large animal practice to be interesting and would go with him when a calf had to be pulled during a cow's difficult birthing.

Most of the horses in our county were mares or geldings. When someone wanted their mare bred, they sometimes would board her in the small fenced area behind the clinic. When Dr. Whaley decided that the mare was ready to be bred, he would call the owner and tell him to arrange for a stud to be brought to the clinic. Stud fees were guaranteed whether or not a foal was conceived, so it was important to make sure that the coupling was successful. A mare in estrus will stand for a stud but the timing is critical. Once the stud arrived, it was my job to hold the mare's halter to calm and steady her as the stud approached. Once studs get the scent of a mare in estrus they can become difficult to control but that was the stud owner's responsibility. They often will bite the mare on the neck during the encounter and an animal that big can hurt the people assisting. It was all over in a few minutes and the stud was taken away much happier than when he first arrived.

Once school started I signed up for the most difficult courses offered in tenth grade. My grades in science and math were good but English continued to be a problem. I rarely did homework. By the time I went to work after school, walked home, ate supper, finished the dishes and bathed on the back porch, I was in no mood to do homework by the dim light of a kerosene lamp. I paid attention in class, had a good memory and managed to pass without too much drama.

In November 1954 our new basketball coach, Cy Lowman, asked me to come out for the team. I said no. My experience with eighth-grade Pony football had not been a good one and I wanted to be sure that I kept my job at the clinic and ranch. I needed the income, but it was a decision that I would later regret.

Uncle Leon never charged me for room and board but he expected me to buy my clothes, pay my school fees, provide lunch money, and cover any other expenses that I might have. He was not a sports fan, and I remembered his admonishment about working when he first told me that I could live with him. I was not about to jeopardize my job or my living arrangement.

My brother, Leon, returned from Gainesville for the Christmas holidays. He split his time between the clinic and the ranch, but I did not see much of him when he was not working. His social life was extensive, and he sometimes did not come home at night. A young man with many girlfriends, he was enjoying the holidays.

Shortly before Christmas, Uncle Leon and I cut a few small sand pine trees and on Christmas Eve we took them to those that he thought might not have one. He had always brought one to Mom before Walter moved in, but did not give her a tree that year. Along with a Christmas tree, he added a live chicken for Christmas dinner and a sack of eggs. He sometimes had brought Mom a new blanket at Christmas, but this year gave one to another family. Blankets were the only store-bought gifts I ever knew him to give.

We did not put up one of the trees, exchange gifts or celebrate the holiday. We instead accepted an invitation for Christmas dinner at Hansel and Ollie Johnson's ranch down at Southport. Ollie's meal was wonderful and we feasted. On the way home we both concluded that Ollie was a better cook than Uncle Leon, and then laughed! My brother, Leon, shared a meal at the Whaley's home.

Winter gave way to spring, and before I knew it, June 1955 had come and I was sixteen years old. A quick trip to the motor vehicle department for my driving demonstration was successful. Suddenly, I could drive when and where I wanted to. Dr. Whaley loaned me the Willys Jeep truck for the test drive and Leon went along in case I did not pass. I now was able to transport myself to and from the ranch in the jeep. There was a deep feeling of independence.

Leon was home for the summer and was again spending most of his time in the clinic. We did not plant grass that year but with the help of a few day-laborers, we did make and store hay. I worked on the ranch most of that summer and enjoyed being in charge of the daily chores. Dr. Whaley was pleased with my work and raised my wage from seventy-five cents to a dollar an hour.

Leon was allowed to drive the Willys Jeep truck home at the end of the work day and I no longer had to walk to and from work.

Dr. Whaley owned a large piece of unimproved land southwest of St. Cloud, and wanted to turn part of it into an orange grove. He directed me to plant several hundred sour orange seeds in rows behind the clinic. I located a large sour orange tree that was laden with fruit and picked them using a tall ladder. The oranges were then cut in half and squeezed, to extract the seeds within. Once the seeds were collected they were washed and dried to make them easier to handle. The seedlings they produced would be grafted with a commercial citrus variety once their stems reached the size of a pencil. Sour orange root-stock had been selected because the property where they were to be planted had a shallow soil profile. In 1955 the planting of the grove was still a few years away but the seedlings were a good start.

In September, Leon returned to the University of Florida for his sophomore year and I began my junior year of high school with a full load of difficult courses. I liked school and now I had extra money to spend. I still had no wheels, but Dr. Whaley started letting me keep the Willys Jeep truck on Friday and Saturday nights during the school year. This assured him that I would be at work on time the following day.

CHAPTER TWENTY-TWO

WHAT HAPPENED WHEN THEY ROLLED UP THE SIDEWALKS?

In late October 1955, Coach Lowman again approached me about trying out for the basketball team. I had grown to nearly 6 feet, 5 inches tall. Being the tallest boy in Osceola High School had piqued his interest. I told him that I would think about it after I talked with Uncle Leon and Dr. Whaley. I did not want to risk losing my job and felt that I needed both of their approvals.

I spoke with Uncle Leon first. He was not a sports fan. Leon had suffered a concussion in football at the beginning of his senior year, and had to be hospitalized for two days of observation. Leon later returned to the team but never performed at the level of his junior year. Uncle Leon paid the hospital bill.

Uncle Leon also was concerned that I might lose my employment. His advice was for me to talk with Dr. Whaley and he agreed to go along with his decision. I would still be able to work Saturdays and Sunday morning.

Dr. Whaley thought that it would be a fine experience and told me that the job would not be jeopardized as long as I continued working on weekends. He was not surprised by the inquiry. Leon had played football, baseball and track during his time in school. I thanked him and reported back to Uncle Leon and Coach Lowman my decision to play that year. I had never held a basketball in my hand or seen a game. I also had not spent much time running. That soon changed.

When the Christmas holiday season arrived, I worked the entire week at the ranch and we practiced basketball at six o' clock each evening. On one occasion that week, I had been doing farm work that left me so dirty that Coach Lowman asked me to take a shower before practice began. It was embarrassing.

Christmas was on Sunday in 1955. I had been paid for a full weeks work on Saturday, Christmas Eve. As I exited the clinic, Dad was waiting for me. I was shocked. I had not seen him since he had laid on the gurney at Lancaster's hospital. He looked gaunt and his hands shook. He said that he had been trying to earn a living peeling grapefruit at a processing plant in Haines City. The fruit were first dipped in hot water to loosen the rind and the work was difficult with his crippled hand. He had been laid off because he could not work fast enough, and asked if I could help. I suspected that he needed the money for whiskey, but felt sorry for him. I took my check across the street to the Army Surplus Store and cashed it. I gave him half of the money and wished him Merry Christmas. He thanked me and then walked away toward town. Christmas day was hard that year.

When I told my brother Leon about the encounter, he gave me a stern lecture and told me to never do that again. He said that he had been down that road before and predicted that Dad would be back. Leon was right. Three weeks later, Dad returned and asked if I could again help him. I told him no. It was the hardest thing that I had ever done. Dad left looking dejected, and I immediately felt guilty.

In January, the two sisters who owned the house that Uncle Leon rented returned for their two-week winter vacation. I moved back into the saddle room to give them the double bed. The meals and housekeeping improved, but they now were deciding whether to put on a new roof. At the end of their stay they left without taking any action.

I spent the first five games on the Junior Varsity team to

learn the game. The other players were younger and at six feet, five inches tall, I was a giant among them. I was also embarrassed to be on the JV team, because the other boys my age were varsity players. The JV team was coached by our math teacher, Hank Ramsey. He was patient and taught me the rules and basic lessons that I needed to be proficient at the game. When the sixth game arrived, I moved up to the varsity and started at the center position. Although never a major threat to score more than ten points, my contributions were in rebounding and closing down the middle of a two-three zone defense.

While other teams used indoor facilities for practice and games, the Osceola High School Kowboy team had only an outdoor, asphalt court. Dribbling was difficult because the court was not completely level, so Coach Lowman had us constantly work on passing drills. When the weather turned cold, the wind was unbearable once you had worked up a sweat. This was a major problem when the coach took you out of the game for a breather. No one could remember a winning season at OHS because it was hard to recruit players under those conditions.

Coach Lowman had bleachers installed on the grass beside the court, and a wooden snow fence surrounded both the bleachers and the basketball court. The school installed lights so that we could play night games. It cost a quarter to enter and sit on the bleachers but people could stand and watch from behind the fence for free. It was the first snow fence that I had ever seen.

At OHS, football was king. The games routinely drew several hundred fans, and were well funded. Basketball was a low budget program. Coach Lowman and Coach Ramsey were determined to change that. We slowly improved and by the end of the season, we had won almost half our games, and people were coming to support us.

Unless you were involved with sports, the sleepy little town of Kissimmee offered a modest amount of nighttime entertainment for teenagers. After they rolled up the sidewalks at seven p.m., the only things left open were the Arcade Theatre, Oren Brown's Pool Hall, a drive-in movie theater at Shingle Creek, and two drive-in hangouts that served teenage appropriate food and drink.

Very few mothers approved of the smoke-filled pool hall, but when one of my friends picked me up in his car, I always found it to be an interesting place to spend time. In addition to recreational pool games, small and big time gambling took place in plain sight, with no interference from the local authorities. I saw a lot of money change hands night after night between players with high skill levels.

Gossip and salty language were common while players waited their turn to shoot. I took it all in, laughing at their jokes and grinning when someone got made fun of, as long as it was not me. In my age group, Keith Padgett was the best player and Leon Fertic was not far behind. Both were better than I was, so I seldom played them for money. Ken Tufts and Pat Lupher rounded out the group of friends and the five of us often did things together.

Two pool tables were reserved for highly skilled players. Nine-ball was played on one table and Keno on the other. Keno was played on a table with the pockets blocked. On one end of the table was a tightly-fitted, polished plywood board with a beveled edge facing the main body of the playing surface. The board had holes the size of the balls with numbers corresponding to the numbered balls.

The game started by racking the number thirteen ball at the front of the rack, and the number fourteen and fifteen balls on the corners. The balls in the interior triangle were then rolled an inch or two back. The player whose turn it was shot the cue ball, striking the thirteen with considerable force. When done properly, the force of the cue ball would propel the fourteen and fifteen balls to bounce off the back rail, strike the side wall of the table and careen over the beveled edge onto the Keno board. When balls landed into a hole that corresponded to the number on the ball, the player earned a Keno, and everyone paid him the agreed upon amount of money. If the ball landed in one of the three holes that had a zero on it, that too was considered a Keno. One hole was marked with two zeros and was worth two Kenos. Everyone took their shots in order. The game ended when someone had a score of fifty points using the combined total of the number on the balls and the number on the holes that each person occupied. The first person to fifty points collected from all the other players. It was a game of great skill and a fair amount of luck. You could lose your shirt in a hurry.

Occasionally, someone would go to Orlando for entertainment. On May 11-12, 1955, "HANK SNOW'S ALL TIME JAMBOREE" was playing at the Orlando Municipal Auditorium. He brought with him several up-and-coming musical stars. Ken Tufts and a few of our friends drove in Ken's 1946 Ford sedan to see the show. I did not go with them because the price of admission was equal to ten hours of hoeing orange trees. When I later asked about the show, someone said that it was good, but one of the opening acts stole the show. "Who was it?" I asked. It took a minute for his reply, but he finally said that it was a funny name, "Elvis, yes that was it." The King had not yet become a national star but his time was near. The girls at the show were calling his name.

At a later date Jerry Lee Lewis came to the Kissimmee and performed in the Community Center near the lakefront. Kids flocked to the performance but once again, I did not buy a ticket. The Center was not air conditioned and when the dancing started, the doors were soon flung open to let some cool air into the building. A dozen or so of us heard and watched the whole concert standing near the entrance. Inside there was "A Whole Lotta Shakin' Going On."

But for the most part, our night time entertainment was

cruising between the Chuck Wagon and the Phil and Nez. The Phil and Nez was strictly a drive-in. It had carhops serving hamburgers, French fries, soft drinks and ice cream sodas. Classmates met, talked, laughed, flirted and changed cars to ride back down main street to the Chuck Wagon and then did it all over again. The routine was always the same. It was reminiscent of the movie "American Pie" and we thought it was fun. I labored under the illusion that if I did that long enough, one of the girls would notice the awkward white-haired beanpole in the passenger seat and smile. It was an unrealized fantasy.

The Chuck Wagon had an indoor dining area with a jukebox that played three songs for a quarter. It was always belting out the latest music and it was there, in February 1956, that I first heard Elvis singing "Heartbreak Hotel". The age of rock and roll had started earlier with Bill Haley and the Comets as well as other artists, but after Elvis, music would never be the same! I instantly became a fan, as did a whole generation of young people.

In up-state New York, the girl that I would eventually meet, fall in love with and marry, was wearing poodle skirts and listening to Pat Boone's "Ain't That A Shame." It was his first hit even though it was a repeat of Fats Domino's version of the same tune. We were geographically and culturally a thousand miles apart.

CHAPTER TWENTY-THREE

THE DARKEST DAY

At the end of the basketball season in my junior year, the players were recognized for their efforts. Letters were awarded to the JV and non-graduating varsity players. Seniors received blue and gold jackets. It was the first institutional recognition that I had ever received. I had not earned a letter in eighth-grade football. I felt good about this new achievement and started looking forward to my senior season.

My life reverted to the routine of going to school and working for Dr. Whaley on the ranch and in the clinic.

On Friday, March 23, 1956, things changed. I came home after work and ate supper, finished the dishes and took my bath on the back porch. I was tired and had no plans to go to town that evening. None of my friends with cars had offered to pick me up. I went to bed early.

At ten thirty, the dogs started barking and woke me up. I heard a car pull up in front of the house. Uncle Leon got up, grabbed his flashlight and shot gun before going outside to see who was arriving that late at night. We did not get many late-night arrivals and he was a cautious man.

He met and recognized the driver and invited him in. A kerosene lamp was lit, and I could hear them talking in low voices. Assuming that it was business related, I stayed in bed and tried to go back to sleep. I never knew who it was that came that night, but later suspected that it had been my Cousin Margie's husband, Paul Bowman. After he left, Uncle Leon came into my room and in a somber voice said, "Your Dad killed himself this evening. I have to go to the funeral home to make arrangements. Do you want to come with me?"

For some reason I said no. It all seemed too unreal. I could not get my head around it. I had seen him a few weeks earlier, and although he looked sad, he gave no indication that he might take his life. I had hurt him with my refusal to help him, and guilt settled over me like a heavy fog. I still could not accept that he was dead. After Uncle Leon left, I lay in bed and second-guessed my decision not to go to the funeral home. Sleep finally beckoned and I did not hear Uncle Leon return later that night.

On Saturday morning, Uncle Leon told me the rest of the macabre story. Dad had prevailed upon my cousin Margie Bacon Bowman and her husband Paul to take Dad to see his wife, Iona, at her home in Haines City.

Dad and Iona had been separated for the past six months, and she had filed for non-support three months earlier. He no longer had a car, and Margie and Paul agreed to provide transportation. On the trip from Kissimmee to Haines City there was no indication of the upcoming violence.

Upon arrival at 8 p.m., Dad went to the porch and began talking with their four pre-school aged children. Margie and Paul remained in the car. After a few minutes, Iona came to the door and the two of them talked for a few minutes before Dad pulled a gun and fired five times at close range. Her most serious injuries were caused by a bullet to her neck and another to her chest. Paul later told police that he then heard a sixth shot and saw Dad fall. He had put the gun in his mouth and pulled the trigger on the sixth and final bullet in the chamber. Dad was later pronounced dead on arrival. Iona would later succumb to her wounds. It was a tragic end to their lives.

Their four children later would be farmed out. Ralph Carl, Junior and Eddie went to live with Iona's parents, and Dee, a three year old boy, and Irene, his two year old sister, were put up for adoption. Forty years later I would meet my half-brother Ralph, but I never again saw the other three. I had only met them briefly. Ralph told me that he later tracked down the fate of two siblings, and learned that they had been placed together in a good home in Jacksonville, Florida. He said that Irene, unfortunately, had been killed in a bicycle collision with an automobile.

I often ask myself, what makes a thirty-seven year old man create so much misery in so many people's lives? Was it genetically preordained? Did it have to happen, or were there forces beyond his control? This man had been a good father and husband before the war. He had worked hard digging ditches for the WPA to support us, and he advanced his career by going to night school to become an electrician. He and my mother had a love affair that was clearly visible to Leon and me. They talked after the evening meal. He supervised our toad hunts. Leon and I listened to them giggle as they washed together at the outdoor water pump. Our parents had friends and we often saw our extended family. He was popular with a wide circle of people who genuinely liked him. I never remember a cross word directed toward my mother before he left for the war. What could have caused him to spiral ever downward, with only brief periods of success and happiness after he came back?

There is little doubt in my mind that it was his experiences in World War II. From the time he returned in February 1946 to his death in March 1956, he could never escape the horrors that he had experienced in war. He relived what he had seen, done and felt in combat. He mourned the loss of his close friend that he had seen gunned down by a volley of machine gun fire. Dad had heard his last moans, watched him twitch and die in the mud. He felt guilty because he had killed a young Japanese soldier at close range and remembered the horror on his face as the young soldier fell into the ravine. He could not forget his own sense of terror during numerous fire-fights, nor could he shake the images of the carnage that he had seen as they advanced toward Luzon. Wounded soldiers with missing limbs, and bodies in the mud. Men calling for a medic. It bothered him that the young soldiers on both sides died so far from home. They would never see their families again. The memories haunted him, and caused him, periodically, to weep and sometimes rage. On the night of March 23, 1956, he had lost all of his sense of humanity.

Dad suffered from uncontrolled survivor's guilt and a severe case of what was then called "Shell Shock". We now call it "Post-Traumatic Stress Syndrome (PTSD)." The memories would haunt him the final ten years of his life. To ease his pain, he turned to whiskey but alcohol only made his problems worse.

By the time he died, Dad had lost his first family and many of his friends who no longer found him to be good company. He could not support himself because of his drinking and his crippled hand. He had alienated himself from Uncle Leon with his behavior, and his children from his first marriage were no longer in his life. He had largely ignored Leon, Denise, and me after he and Mom divorced, and he had driven me away when he dropped me off at Grandpa Will's home in August 1950. He was estranged from Iona, and faced possible arrest for non-support of their children. To make matters worse, he had heard rumors that Iona had been seeing her first husband during their separation.

He was totally alone and could no longer cope with life. Years earlier, in a drunken rage, he had tried to shoot Mom, and had failed. By all accounts he was not drinking this night, but he succeeded in mortally wounding Iona. She would die eight months later on Wednesday, November 14, 1956, after spending the entire time in the Polk County Hospital.

I ask myself, how could Dad reconcile shooting Iona at close range, when it had tortured him to remember killing the young Japanese soldier at a similar distance?

It was a great tragedy. I had not spent much time with Iona, but I liked her. She had always been kind. Now there were four young children with no parents. It had taken ten years, but the experiences of war had ultimately exacted an unspeakable toll on two entire families. And on this night, the war had killed once again.

CHAPTER TWENTY-FOUR

SABRA - AN OLD FLAME

For Dad's funeral, I borrowed a suit from a friend who played basketball with me. I had never bought myself nice clothes, but felt that I should not go wearing jeans. My brother, Leon, was away at the university and did not attend, but I was aware that if he did, he would be nicely dressed. He took a great deal of pride in his appearance and had been voted "best dressed" in his senior year of high school. It was just one of the many accolades for which he had been recognized. Uncle Leon put on the only tie that I ever saw him wear, and helped me make a proper knot in the tie that I had borrowed.

I was surprised when I walked into the Chapel at Grissom's Funeral Home on the following Monday. Although Dad had committed an especially heinous act, there was standing room only. I thought it strange that so many had come to see him buried, when in life, we had all drifted away.

After the Reverend D. D. Debault completed his service, Dad was laid to rest at Pleasant Hill Cemetery. He received a military service burial and afterward Uncle Leon was given the flag that draped his coffin. At a later date, Uncle Leon would sign the request for a military headstone.

I tried, but could not hold back my tears. I never understood the man, but he was my Dad, and I felt a sense of loss. I was not sure if my tears were in mourning for him or for the simple realization that the shadow that he cast over our family was finally gone. His downward spiral had taken ten years and he had suffered greatly with his memories but he also had caused much anguish and pain to those who had once loved and admired him. Now it was over and I felt numb to the reality. Somehow I would have to find closure.

When I went to school on Tuesday, everyone knew the story. Classmates did not know what to say to me. Teachers suggested that I take a day or two off to mourn. I thanked them for their concern, but said that I preferred to attend classes. It was awkward.

After school, I went to the clinic and Dr. Whaley told me to take the week off. "Come back Saturday," he said. I decided to do as he suggested. His suggestion was not unusual. When the work was caught up at the ranch, and if the clinic was not busy, he was up front about shorting my after-school hours.

A week after Dad's death his obituary was on page 7 of the Friday, March 30, 1956 edition of the Kissimmee Gazette.

"Local Man Shoots Wife, Kills Self
Ralph Carl Allen Is Suicide, Wife In Critical Condition

A 37 year-year old Kissimmee electrician rode to Haines City, with friends, Friday night, to see his children and estranged wife then shot her five times and killed himself while the friends watched from their car.

The wife, Mrs. Iona May Allen was in critical condition Friday night at Polk County Hospital, Bartow. Her most serious wounds were one in the neck and one in the chest.

Dead, police reported, was Ralph Carl Allen.

The couple had been separated about six months.

Kissimmee Couple

Patrolmen Ellis Green and Harold Partin said that Allen was brought to his wifes home on Pinner Avenue, Haines City, at 8 PM Friday by Mr. and Mrs. Paul Bowman 511 Bay street, Kissimmee.

The couple told police Allen went to the porch of his wife's home and was talking to their four pre-school age children when Mrs. Allen came to the door.

Police said Bowman told them the couple talked a few minutes then Allen pulled a gun and fired five times, and his wife slumped to the porch floor. Bowman said the he heard another shot and saw Allen fall.

Allen was pronounced dead on arrival at the Green-Roberts clinic at Haines City of a gunshot wound in the mouth.

The Bowmans told officers that Allen gave no indication of committing any violence during the trip from Kissimmee to Haines City. Police said Mrs. Allen had charged Allen with non-support three months ago.

A native of Kissimmee, he was a lifelong resident.

He was a veteran of World War II, and a member of the Baptist Church. He was an electrician.

Survivors include his wife Iona Andrews Allen, Haines City; his parents W.H. Allen, Indian River City, and Mrs. Ruby Perfitt, of Kissimmee; three sons, Leon H. Allen and William A. Allen, Kissimmee, and Ralph Carl Allen Jr. of Haines City; two daughters, Denise Allen, Kissimmee, Irene Allen, Haines City; One sister, Mrs. Hal Register, Jr., Mount Dora; two Brothers W. C. Allen, Kissimmee and Clifton Allen, Goldenrod.

Funeral services were held at 2 PM Monday from Grissom Chapel, with the Rev. D. D .Debault, Pastor of the First Christian Church, officiating. Casket bearers were Dee Bronson, Buster Patrick, Earl Lamb, Oren Brown, and Harry Tuft. Interment was in Pleasant Hill Cemetery; Grissom Funeral Home in Charge."

Life returned to normal after that week. I had the suit that I had borrowed dry-cleaned and returned it to its owner. On Saturday, I checked in at Whaley's Clinic and worked from eight to five. That night I went cruising with my friends.

In April, I again had a week with no after-school work. When classes were over, I went home and was surprised to find a woman sitting in her car in front of the house. Uncle Leon was not home. "Are you Bill?" she asked. I replied that I was and asked who she was. "I'm Sabra. I'm an old friend of your

Uncle Leon."

I invited her to come in the house, and she told me that she and Uncle Leon had been friends when they were younger. I guessed that she was about his same age. She was medium height, a little overweight and had colored her hair an auburn tint. She asked me about school and we talked until Uncle Leon returned home.

When his truck rolled to a stop, Uncle Leon was greeted by his two tail- wagging dogs that sniffed and rubbed against him. He walked into the house and hung his hat on the cow-horn hat rack near the door. He was surprised but pleased at seeing Sabra sitting on the couch. She got up and hugged him.

"What in the world are you doing back in Kissimmee?" he asked.

"My husband died a few months back and I'm spending some time with family. I had some time on my hands and thought that I would visit old friends. There's not many that I know anymore. Most have died or moved away. Belle told me that you were still here."

I was not a part of the conversation so I went out to feed the livestock and to collect eggs. When I finished, I sat on the back porch and petted the dogs who were now well-fed and very mellow.

In the house, Sabra and Uncle Leon were deep in conversation. He invited her to stay for dinner and she accepted. They continued talking while he prepared the meal, and she set the table. I stayed out of the way. They were enjoying each other's company. After dinner, he walked her to the car while I washed and dried the dishes.

I did not see her again for several days, but they later started spending time together. Sabra always drove because she had a car and he only had his cattle truck.

That summer, Uncle Leon received a letter informing him that the two sisters had decided to sell the property that he had been renting for many years. They had concluded that they no longer wanted to be responsible for the upkeep in their advancing years. Shortly thereafter, we moved into a house that Uncle Leon purchased from Joe Fertic.

The new house was located in a highland hammock near the spot that once had been Pinky Villa, a juke joint popular with soldiers during the war. The house was much smaller than the one we had previously occupied. It had two bedrooms, a living room, and a kitchen. A bathroom had been roughed in, but was not finished. There were no bathroom fixtures nor was it connected to a septic system. Small front and back porches completed the structure. The house had electricity and an electric pump that provided cold running water to a spigot on the back porch and to a sink in the kitchen. A small barn, a chicken coop, and an outhouse were located a short distance behind the house.

The house was surrounded with a dense forest of oak trees and brush that let not a breath of breeze penetrate to the small clearing around the house. The hammock was high ground, surrounded by large expanses of grass land. We soon learned that when the summer rains came, snakes from the pasture land moved into the hammock. Night time trips to the outhouse required a large flash light and Uncle Leon always carried his 410 pistol with him to dispatch rattle snakes.

Fortunately, I had bought a 1931 four-door Chevrolet sedan in May, or I would have been isolated that summer. The car was older than me and was in poor condition. I paid $45 for the car, which came with four additional bald tires that were showing their threads. Ninety percent of the top of the auto was covered with canvas that leaked over the driver's seat when it rained. The cloth seats smelled a little musty. The engine cut off when you removed your foot from the gas pedal to brake. Top speed was forty miles an hour. I loved it! It was wheels, and I was mobile!

Surely now I could find a girlfriend. I asked two girls to go out and both said no before hanging up the phone. It was obvious that neither of them had read the manual on how to let a boy down easy. As it turned out, all the girls seemed to be more interested in boys with newer cars with glass-pack mufflers. Maybe my car was not the answer!

When I first brought the car home, Uncle Leon was amused and asked me "why did you buy this one?" "It only cost forty-five dollars," was my answer. "And it reminded me of Grandma Ruby's Model-A car that she took all of us kids in when she went to buy coal oil for her stove."

"Hell boy, that was not coal oil, it was moonshine," he snorted. "Ruby bought it in gallon jugs, then cut and resold it in pint jars. She knew that no one would stop an old woman with a bunch of kids in her car." I stood there not knowing whether I should be shocked or proud of her business acumen. I did remember that she bought several jugs at a time, and I also knew that she had no visible means of support beyond her garden, fruit trees and a milk cow. We kids were merely cover for a Cracker woman with a plan.

Sabra moved in later that summer. I came home from work and she was preparing a meal for the three of us. Her clothes had been unpacked and she had a big glass of iced, cherry Kool-Aid waiting for me. After working in the field all day, it hit the spot. It was a treat that she made for me every day that summer.

A few months later she started referring to herself as Sabra Allen. I never knew if they were legally married, nor did I ask.

Sabra took over the housework. She was an excellent cook and Sunday meals were once again special. She and I washed the dishes together every night. Once a week, she washed our clothes on a rub board and I would hold the basket of the wet clean clothes, while she hung them on the clothes line to dry. We got comfortable with one another, and I started calling her "Aunt Sabra." I think that she liked that.

Aunt Sabra asked very little of me during the five summers that we all lived together. We ate a steady diet of beef and chicken, but she liked fried fish. About once a week she would ask me to stop after work and catch a few bass for supper. I was eager to accommodate her. After a long day in the sun, I would wade out into the cooling water of Lake Tohopekaliga and throw a small gold lure along the weed line. It seldom took more than thirty minutes to catch enough for our meal.

After a few months, Aunt Sabra took a job ironing clothes at the local laundry. She wanted to have her own money. She installed a telephone, and within a year, she added a television set. The phone gave her access to her friends and family, but for Uncle Leon it was nothing but a nuisance. He would not use it. Instead he would drive twenty miles to talk business, as he had always done. He quickly warmed to the TV. We watched the evening news and the Ed Sullivan Show but his favorite program was Gunsmoke.

Aunt Sabra's pin money soon became the only thing that ever caused friction between them. Uncle Leon had diabetes and had given up drinking many years before. Sabra liked gin. She would buy half pints and hide them in the house. Once or twice each week, after supper, she would return to her cache, and drink the whole bottle at one time. I witnessed her do this on two occasions. Within minutes she would be slurring her words and falling asleep in her chair. Although he disapproved of her drinking, he would gently put her to bed.

I was never sure whether or not they loved each other, or if their union was simply a matter of needing someone in their life. He had never been married. Sabra had survived multiple marriages. They would remain together until his death in December, 1966.

CHAPTER TWENTY-FIVE

COLLEGE AND PURE SERENDIPITY

My senior year flew by with the usual routine of classes and work. Our once powerful football team lost most of their games. And in a tragic turn of events, our quarterback, Mike Treat, was tackled and badly injured. He was flown to New York for treatment but subsequently became a quadriplegic for the rest of his life. While in New York, some of the team members drove up to lift his spirits. A popular kid, Mike was not only an athlete; he was also the class Vice-President.

Basketball season had better success. For the first time that anyone could remember, we won more than half of our games. One of the coaches said that it was the first winning season in the history of the program. Cy Lowman and Hank Ramsey had turned the program around in less than four years, and everyone felt good about what we had accomplished. The following year I was told that the team won the conference title.

There were only a few games that stick in my mind. At the beginning of the season, I was selected to be the captain for the first game. I had never received such an important honor and felt on top of the world. Coach Lowman told me to bring my mother for the opening ceremony.

I had kept in touch with Mom while living with Uncle Leon. On days when Dr. Whaley had no work for me, I often dropped by Hansel's Citrus Packing Plant where she was now working. Unable to do the heavy lifting required at the crate mill, she had quit work when Walter came to live with us in

1953. She now assembled cardboard boxes for shipping fresh fruit. Each box was folded together and stapled using a foot-operated stapling machine. On my visits, I would assemble boxes and hand them to her for stapling while we talked. It was piece-work and she appreciated the help.

They had left Aultman Island, and were now living in one of the better houses on the road to the stockyards. It was a great improvement over the house that we had earlier lived in.

When I asked her to come to the game I was surprised that she said no. When I inquired why, she gave me no answer. I persisted, and she finally agreed to come if I would pick her up and pay her way into the game. In later years, I realized that she probably felt uncomfortable because her wardrobe was limited. I agreed to her request, but had to tell my coach that I would be late for the warm-up. He said that he understood but he was not happy. I realized that I had failed the test of team leadership. The captain was not supposed to be late.

In mid-season my brother, Leon, stopped by to watch a game. He had not returned to college, citing money problems. Leon was now working for a propane delivery service. He had an apartment and I rarely saw him about town. Never a prolific scorer, I scored eighteen points and dominated the boards that night. Every ball that I threw up seemed to find the basket. Having never seen me play, he concluded that my skill level was higher than it was. It was the most points that I ever scored in a game, and I was glad that he had been there to see it.

Uncle Leon and Aunt Sabra sometimes would park in the parallel parking spaces, about seventy five feet from the outdoor court, and watch the game from the car. He would never come over to the court where we were playing, but it made me happy to see the old black and white Chevy, and to know that they were there.

As with every sports activity the last game is the hardest. We made the regional playoffs, but were seeded last in the tournament against the number one seed, the Daytona Seabreeze Sandcrabs. At the end of regulation, to everyone's surprise, we were tied. They beat us in overtime.

I had not shed tears since Dad's funeral. There was suddenly a huge hole in my life. I did not want the season to end. I had been a major part of the team. Together we had a winning season and changed the course of basketball at Osceola High School. It was the only time in high school that I had felt a part of something important, and I already missed it.

In the spring of 1957, some of my classmates were being called in for college counseling. They were the kids who had been the best students and class leaders. They had demonstrated that they were prepared for college. Most of them had family financial support. Although I had taken the most difficult curriculum offered at the school, I did not project well on the scale being used to measure college potential. My teachers knew that I had no financial support.

Fortunately, my good friend, Leon Fertic, did see the counselor. While there, he picked up two applications to the University of Florida and later handed one to me and said, "Hey Bill, let's go to college." I sent in the application a few days later and before the school year was over, I had been accepted. One of the most important decisions of my life had been pure chance, and I was the better for it. Now all I needed to do was to figure out how to pay for it.

I had seen my brother start college, run out of money after three semesters and have to leave the university. Leon had sold his horse and worked hard in the summer for Dr. Whaley to earn money. He told me that he and another student had lived in an apartment at the animal science facility to provide security for the animals. His presence at the farm meant that he paid no rent. It still had not been enough to keep him in school. I began laying plans to avoid his fate.

I told Dr. Whaley that I had been accepted by the University of Florida and asked if I could count on full employment that summer. He readily agreed. I then told him that I wanted to turn in my hours each week to the bookkeeper, and be paid in one lump sum at the end of the summer. I would take a five dollar draw each week for spending money. The 1931 Chevy had not turned out to be the chick magnet that I had hoped for; so much to my chagrin, money for dates was not needed.

When I was in the tenth grade, one of Uncle Leon's cows had died, leaving a heifer calf that was too young to survive on its own. He planned to shoot it to end its misery. At the last minute, he had paused and asked me if I wanted to try to care for it. I jumped at the chance to have my own calf. We loaded it in the truck and took it home. On the way home we stopped at Lou Tarcai's farm store and bought a bucket with a rubber nipple and a supply of powdered milk.

In the summer of 1957, the little red calf was now nearly two years old and pastured with Uncle Leon's herd. In the not too distant future, she would be producing a calf.

Once I had the first calf, I wanted another. During my junior year, Walter had bought four Holstein dairy calves to take advantage of the grass at Aultman Island. They had just been weaned, and were small. Three of them were bull calves but one was a heifer. Having over-extended himself, he offered to sell me one of the calves. I chose the heifer and bought a hundred pound sack of feed to get her off to a good start. Mom suggested that the calf stay with them because of the abundant pasture. She fed my calf along with hers for the first two months, and then Uncle Leon and I picked up the calf, and took her to pasture with his herd. In another few years, she too would be calving. Both cows would play an important part in my college finances.

Now all I needed was a job while I was at school. One day while having lunch at Margie's restaurant on Main Street, Margie's son, David McGonigal, told me that his older brother, Eddie, was finishing his degree at the University of Florida. He had worked as a manager for the football team and that position was available. I asked for the name and address of the person that I needed to get in touch with. "Sarge Bannister. He is the equipment manager" was the reply. I wrote him the next day and soon learned that the job was mine. It paid fifty dollars a month. I wrote back and accepted the job.

Housing was the next challenge. The school counselor recommended that my friend Leon Fertic, apply to the Georgia Seagle Hall near the campus. Leon and I left for Gainesville a few days later in his father's car. The one hundred and twenty five mile trip to Gainesville was the farthest that I had ever been from Kissimmee.

When we arrived at the Georgia Seagle Hall, it was almost lunchtime. A house member handed us paperwork to be filled out and then went in to eat. His demeanor was cold and off-putting. While the members ate, we filled out the application. When I got to the part at the bottom of the application that asked for a signed pledge that I would not smoke, drink or gamble, I looked over at Leon and said, "Lets get out of here." I didn't smoke but the drinking and gambling pledge seemed a bridge too far. We left and went to see a friend, Davis Bateman, who was living at the Cooperative Living Organization (CLO). There we received a warm welcome and lunch. We filled out the necessary paperwork and became members the following September.

I had put all of the pieces together, with only a long, hot summer of field work left.

CHAPTER TWENTY-SIX

WORKING FOR THE GATORS

In late August 1957, I packed my clothes in one of Aunt Sabra's old suitcases and Uncle Leon drove me to Gainesville to start my new life as a Gator at the University of Florida. It was the first time my clothes had ever been packed in anything but a paper bag. It was drizzling when we arrived at the Cooperative Living Organization (CLO). Uncle Leon pulled up in front of the brick building, wished me well and drove away. Neither he nor Aunt Sabra got out of the car. He wanted to be sure that he was home when it was time to feed the livestock.

In my wallet was a certified bank check for $404. It was the total sum of the money that I had to start college. I had saved my hours that summer and cashed them in the week before. Dr. Whaley's bookkeeper had suggested that I use a bank check because a personal check may take a day or two to clear in Gainesville.

The few students that were at CLO were surprised to see me. School did not start for three more weeks. I explained that I was required to be at two-a-day football practices which started in two days. After lunch at a local cafeteria, I opened a bank account and made my way to the team's locker room to meet Sarge Bannister. A short, middle-aged man with thinning brown hair, he quickly put me at ease and explained my duties and the work schedule. When he asked about my luggage, I told him that I left it at CLO. "Go get it. You will be sleeping in the dorms with the team until classes start."

I retrieved my suit case and reported back. Players were

also checking in when I got my room assignment. Along with pillows and sheets, I was given a large alarm clock. It was my responsibility to make sure all players on my floor were awake at 6 o'clock every morning. Rising at 5:45 a.m., I would walk down the hall banging on every player's door. "Six o'clock. Wake up. Rise and shine." Other managers had similar responsibilities on different floors. Early morning wake-up duty did not make the managers popular with the players, especially the freshmen, who were accustomed to being treated like stars in their home towns.

During the preseason training period managers were allowed to eat at the player's training table. I had never seen so much food and it was all the best cuts of meat and produce. Like all of the players, I feasted at the buffet three times a day.

Before each practice session, managers passed out clean practice jerseys, pants and socks. Sarge washed yesterday's practice uniforms while the players and managers were on the field. Other managers had responsibility for setting up the pads on blocking machines, making sure that there were enough balls and that the balls were properly inflated.

The pace of practice was brutal. Players ran between practice stations with little or no down time. The summer heat and humidity were stifling. Players who reported out of condition threw up. Practices were highly organized, and the players were exhausted at day's end. So were the managers because we worked longer hours than the players. After each practice some managers went inside to retrieve practice uniforms while others secured the equipment that could otherwise be stolen or vandalized. Everyone cleaned the locker room after the players had finally left the building.

Once classes began, the managers moved out of the dorm where we had been living and we could no longer eat at the training table. I returned to CLO and shared a room with Leon Fertic and a new kid from Clearwater, Elmer Williams. The three of us soon become fast friends.

Freshmen practiced with the varsity team, but had a separate game schedule. By the time that we played our first freshman game, I had been made head manager of the three freshman managers and was responsible for making sure that everything was in place for the game. We traveled by train to play Tulane that year. I had not been on a train since our class trip to Orlando, when I was in elementary school.

The day before we left, Sarge told me that I needed to wear a coat and tie for the trip. I had neither. When I got back to the CLO that night, I let some of the members know about my dilemma. Someone volunteered a checkered sports coat that had been left by a previous member. Another member loaned me dress slacks and a third person gave me a very loud, wide tie. Nothing matched or fit well. I looked like a clown. I arrived at the locker room ready to help make final arrangements for the trip. Sarge was in disbelief at what he was seeing. "Is that all that you have to wear," he inquired? I told him that it was and that I had borrowed the clothes. He shook his head and summoned me to follow him. He took me back to where the team's traveling uniforms were stored and picked slacks and a coat that fit. He then handed me a Gator tie and told me to get some better shoes before the next trip. They were the finest clothes that I had ever put on my body and they felt good. After that, I was the only manager that wore the official Gator traveling uniform. Sarge had figured out my situation and was determined to not let it become a problem for me or the team.

The Gator freshman team won the game that afternoon, and the coaches scheduled time for us to see a little of New Orleans before we left the next morning. I and a trainer were responsible for passing out meal money after the game. Each player, trainer, and manager got ten dollars which was a princely sum for me. A tight end from the team and I made our way down to Bourbon Street and soon found a bar that would sell beer to two underage kids. While we sat nursing a beer, we were surprised that the curtain behind the bar suddenly opened. A beautiful young woman began to dance and take off some of her clothing. I had never seen such a thing, but I knew that I was no longer in Kissimmee! I had been in college only a few weeks, and was already getting an education!

When classes started, it did not take long for me to realize that I was in deep trouble. Although I had taken the most difficult courses in high school, I was not at the level of most freshmen. I seldom had done more home work than was absolutely necessary. I used study hall for the purpose that it was intended, and usually could find a classmate to help with English. That practice had lowered my grade point, but I was content to be a B student in most subjects. Math and science were different. I made A's in those courses and it satisfied Uncle Leon. When I had brought my first report card home in the fall of 1954, I had made the honor roll with all B's. I was pleased with those grades, but he was not.

"Boy, if you want to be able to make a living, you need to be better than everyone else at something! I want to see an A on your next report card." Wanting to please him, I concentrated on math and science, which for me were the easiest courses. Unfortunately, I neglected English grammar.

Standardized tests were administered at the start of the semester, and my language deficiency was immediately discovered. The results were handed back in the Comprehensive English Course by the instructor, Mr. Key, who commented on each score so that everyone could hear. "Great score Miss Jones. I hope that you will be majoring in literature. Good work Mr. Johnson. You have a bright future." When he got to me he raised his voice. "Mr. Allen. Well, here's another one that won't make it." It was humiliating. I was told to report to the Remedial Writing Lab, where I labored for the remainder of the semester. In the end, the instructor liked the stories that I wrote and let me pass out of the class. I had not progressed to the point that I needed to, but at least I was moving on.

Because I was working for the football team, I was given preferential class scheduling. Players, trainers and managers were allowed to choose our classes before the other students, so that we could be finished with classes by lunchtime. My classes started at 7:40 each morning and classes ran continuously until 12:40 p.m. I ran back to CLO, gobbled down my lunch, and reported for work by 1:30 p.m. Our work day was over by 7 o'clock after the last player had left the locker room and we had finished getting ready for the next day.

After work I walked back to the CLO where Jesse, the cook, had a plate of food waiting in the oven. His wife and sister worked with him, and while the women were cleaning up from the evening meal, he was reading scripture to them. By simple proximity, I was a part of his congregation, as he practiced his weekly church sermon. Jesse was a preacher and by the sermons that I heard, he was a good one. After dinner I retired to my desk to study until midnight. There was no time for anything else. I quickly realized that I should have signed up for fewer than eighteen hours of classes.

The University of Florida is a Land-Grant University. President Lincoln signed the Land-Grant College Act of 1862, or Morrill Act, shortly before his assassination. The act provided land to each state to establish a college that would educate the common people. Prior to the Act being signed, education was for children of wealthy families.

Land-Grant Universities are required to teach Agriculture, Engineering and Military Science. In 1957, the Reserve Officer Training Corp (ROTC) was required of all male students in their freshman and sophomore years, as a means of meeting the requirement for Military Science Training.

I was no exception to that requirement. Like so many others before me, I quickly learned to march, stand at attention, take orders and spit shine my army issue shoes.

Everything was new and coming at me very fast, but I was surviving. Surely it had to get better.

In October 1957, everyone's world changed. The Soviet Union put a satellite in space. Its name was Sputnik. At night it was possible to see its blinking light crossing the sky. There was suddenly a national panic that the Soviets could put an atomic bomb on a satellite and we could do nothing about it. Congress realized that we needed to catch up with the Soviets and in October of 1958, passed the National Defense Education Act (NDEA). The act authorized scholarship loan funds for students majoring in science, math, and education. The cold war was in full swing, and in space, the Soviet Union was winning.

I survived that first semester with all C's. It was enough to keep my job so that I had money to stay in school. To be employed as a manager it was necessary to maintain a 2.0 GPA on a 4.0 scale. In English, I had survived by 2 points on a 1,000-point scale.

The second semester was easier. I still worked for the football team, but the hours were fewer. There were only a few weeks of spring practice and the rest of the time we did whatever Sarge asked us to do. It was mostly make-work projects. In between projects we were free to shoot baskets in the gym and play pickup basketball games. Although we still reported for work at one thirty, we were usually done by 4 PM.

The football locker room was attached to the basketball gym and it was common to have Gator basketball players playing pickup games in the gym, once their season was over. The managers often joined in with them, when Sarge allowed. I played as often as I could. My scoring was not good, but my defense got me noticed by the basketball coach. He asked me to try out for the team. I told him that I really wanted to, but I needed the money the manager's job provided. I asked him if he could arrange a dorm room and meals at the training table. I would cover tuition, fees and books. He said that he was unable to provide that until I earned a scholarship. He was looking for a scrimmage horse and I knew that my offensive skills would guarantee that I would never see the court during a game. I thanked him for asking but declined his offer. My manager's job provided my only means of financial support and I could not take a chance.

During my sophomore year, I was made head manager for the varsity team. The responsibility earned me an additional $20 per month. I was now making $70 every payday and I enjoyed the recognition accorded to me. Varsity trips were more exciting.

On October 8, 1958, the Gator football team flew a charter flight to Los Angeles to play UCLA. It was the first time that I traveled on an airplane. We left shortly before dark on Wednesday with a refueling stop scheduled in Houston, Texas. I was nervous about flying but everything was going well until it got dark. It was then that I looked out the window and saw a three-foot-long flame come out of the engine on the right wing of the airplane. I hit the call button and a flight attendant came to my seat and asked what I wanted. "The engine is on fire," I said while pointing for the flight attendant. She looked out the window at the plane's engine, then back at me and smiled. This is your first flight isn't it?" she said. I felt like a real rube and asked for a coke.

She checked on me a lot during the flight and when we arrived, I gave her and another attendant my two tickets to the game.

The Gators won that historic night game on Friday the 10th by a score of 21-14. It was the first time that the Gators had played against a black player. A few years later, the Southeast Conference would break the color barrier against black athletes and become the dominant football conference in the country. As Bob Dylan implied in his song, "Times, They Are A-Changin."

CHAPTER TWENTY-SEVEN

LEAVING THE COOPERATIVE LIVING ORGANIZATION

I stopped working for the football team in November 1958, just before the last game. I had not learned the lesson about scheduling too many classes and my grades were suffering in two courses. Unencumbered with work, my grades quickly recovered, but my finances were now suffering. I began applying for small need-based scholarships and was awarded two that totaled less than $125. It was enough to get me to Christmas. I suddenly realized that I was on the same financial path as my brother Leon had been when he dropped out of the university.

Hearing that the NDEA scholarship loans were now available, I put in an application in November.

When the semester break came that year I was out of money. I decided that I would not return to campus after the break. Instead I would go home, work and save money, and be back the next September.

I packed my clothes and other personal items and waited for my ride home. Freshmen and sophomores at the university were not allowed to have automobiles, so I had relied upon Davis Bateman for rides to and from Kissimmee. He generously allowed me to travel with him in his pickup truck.

There was only one rule; he would not wait two minutes after the announced time of departure. If our schedules did not mesh, he left on his schedule. On two occasions, I could not make the schedule from Kissimmee to Gainesville and wound up thumbing a ride. Uncle Leon drove me to the Citrus Tower in Clermont and I would use a cardboard sign that simply said "Gainesville." In those days it never took long for a kid to get a ride to college on Highway 27.

I had my bag and boxes packed and waiting next to the truck at the time Davis had said that we would leave. "What are the boxes for," he inquired?'

"I'm not coming back. I am out of money."

We discussed my situation for a few minutes with Davis trying to talk me into leaving my possessions in my room and reconsidering after the break. I had made up my mind and Davis finally said OK. After loading my boxes and suitcase into the back of his truck I suddenly remembered that I had not checked my mail and ran quickly inside. There in my mailbox was an envelope announcing that I had been awarded an NDEA scholarship loan. I let out a whoop, told Davis the good news and he insisted that I take my boxes back to my room. He said that he would not leave until I did. I believe that it was the only time he had ever waited for anyone.

When I got home, Dr. Whaley gave me a few days work, and Uncle Leon gave me a substantial check. He had sold my first yearling a few days earlier. Suddenly everything looked a lot rosier.

The years flew by. At the end of my sophomore year, Leon, Elmer, Sagid Salahutin and I left CLO and moved into a second floor two bedroom, off-campus apartment. Sagid was older than the other three of us. He was an ethnic Turk that had grown up in Seoul, South Korea. His father had been a merchant and the whole family was taken prisoner when North Korean soldiers captured Seoul in June 1950. He had survived three years in a North Korean prison camp.

Leon and Sagid cooked, and Elmer and I washed dishes. Leon's cooking was what one might expect from a college student, but Sagid's food was so spicy that it sometimes was too hot to eat. Sagid said that he had learned to eat spicy food in the concentration camp. He speculated that the North Koreans made their food extra hot so that their prisoners would not eat too much. He said that he had adjusted and liked it that way. I had developed an ulcer at the end of my sophomore year and Sagid's food was sometimes a real hurdle.

Early in the first semester of our junior year, Elmer arrived at the apartment with a baby squirrel in his shirt pocket. It had apparently fallen out of its nest onto the sidewalk and was squeaking. It was clearly unable to survive on its own, so Elmer decided to take care of the newborn. He fed it milk using an eyedropper and the squirrel grew very fast. Soon we were all feeding it raw peanuts, which it begged for constantly. We never let it outside, but it had full run of the apartment. We thought of it as a pet until it become an adult and developed an annoying habit that led to its banishment. It suddenly started slipping up behind everyone but Elmer, and peeing on them. After this happened more than once, we gave Elmer an ultimatum that the squirrel had to go. Elmer put the squirrel outside and he climbed a tree. The squirrel was not missed by anyone except Elmer.

At the beginning of my junior year, Leon Fertic and I decided to stay in ROTC and become Army officers. Elmer, who had completed his obligation, decided that he had enough of ROTC and chose not to continue. Cadets in officer training are required to go for basic training at the end of their junior year. When I reported for my physical, I had to tell the attending physician that I had an ulcer. The doctor closed his notebook and declared me unfit for service. I left disappointed that I would not be commissioned. I also really needed the $27 a month that cadets were paid in their third and fourth year of ROTC.

Being dropped from the ROTC program may have saved my life. In all class activities cadets lined up in the same prescribed order. When I left the program, the cadet next in line behind me, moved into my spot. I was told that during that summer, he was killed in a training exercise by a lightning strike. Assigned to be a radioman that day, he had raised his antenna in a thunderstorm.

Following my junior year, Sagid graduated and left the apartment. Elmer married his long time girlfriend, Martha Lee, in the summer of 1960 and I was his best man. It was the first wedding that I had ever seen. Elmer, Martha, Leon and I shared an apartment the first semester of our senior year to save money. At mid-year, Leon married our high school classmate and friend, Judy Rollins, on New Year's Eve, 1960. I felt honored to be a part of their wedding. They moved to an apartment across the street. I stayed and shared the apartment with Elmer and Martha.

For the first three years at the university I had majored in Agricultural Education and was preparing to become a Vocational Agricultural Teacher. I enjoyed the broad curriculum of courses in agriculture but was growing dissatisfied with the education courses. During the second semester of my junior year, Entomology was a required course for agriculture. I had put off the course as long as I could, thinking I would not like it. I was wrong. I found out what every ten-year old boy instinctively knows: insects are fascinating. Three weeks after the course began, I decided to change my major to Entomology.

I now faced a dilemma. To earn a degree in Entomology, it was necessary for the student to pass sixteen required courses and I wanted to finish in four years. Although the NDEA loans were propping me up financially, my accumulating debt was larger than I wanted.

At the end of my junior year I scheduled a meeting with the Department Head and discussed my dilemma. He said that it normally took two years to complete the curriculum. I told him that I could not find enough money to stay that long, and that I wanted to finish in one year. We talked for a while before he relented and said, "Well if you are determined to try, I suppose that I won't try to stop you."

In the first semester of my senior year I signed up for nine Entomology courses. I had already earned enough general agricultural credits. I took no employment that semester and the schedule was brutal. I walked from one class to another in a haze from late night studying. Tests were often back-to-back. I studied until the local radio station played Santos and Johnny's recording of "Sleep Walk" and the National Anthem before they signed off at midnight.

When I returned to Kissimmee over Christmas Break, Dr. Whaley told me that he had no work for me. It was the first time that I was out of a job since I enrolled at the university. I needed the two weeks of pay, so I started asking around. By the second week, the only response that I had was from the Cooperative Extension Agricultural Agent, June Gunn. He said that he had a day's work repairing rusty fences on his ranch. I took the job and at the end of the day he handed me $8. It was not all that I needed but it was a start. I continued to ask around but had no luck.

Two days before I was scheduled to return to Gainesville, I stopped in at Brown's pool room to see if any of my friends were there. They were not, so I started watching four heavy-weight pool sharks playing Keno with a much less talented player. The game was fifty cent Keno. The fish was hooked and losing because he was in over his head, and did not realize it. I watched the game for about twenty minutes before deciding to join when the rotation would place me behind the fish. It was a good decision. The player that I followed continued to leave me good shots and I often was able to put multiple balls on the board with a single stroke of my cue stick. Luck is a big part of a Keno game. Like the player that I followed, I was far less talented than the four heavyweights, but for the next three hours I could not miss. Every numbered ball found a good hole and I was stealing breaks and making Kenos. By the time the game broke up, I had won over eighty dollars which was more than the two weeks wages I was hoping to earn. It was a big night. I had never won more than two dollars at any time while playing pool.

In the spring I signed up for the final seven courses. With a slightly diminished course load, I took a job at the Florida Department of Agriculture and Consumer Services, Division of Plant Industry, supporting Dr.Wally Dekle's program. Wally had been trapping insects in the Dry Tortugas and needed help sorting and classifying his catch. The insects that were caught in his light traps were stored in quart bottles and preserved in alcohol. My job was to sort the insects to Order and Family, and take a count of each. The research was mind numbing work, but it was a pay check.

In June 1961, I graduated along with Leon and Judy Fertic. Elmer would have to wait another year to complete his degree.

Dr. Whaley and his wife Patsy drove up and attended the graduation ceremony. Afterwards they took Elmer, Martha and me to lunch. They were surprised that neither Uncle Leon and Aunt Sabra, nor Mom and Walter came. Mom later said that she and Walter had taken my siblings to pick tomatoes in Estero, Florida. They needed the money, and it was a wise choice.

With the NDEA loan program, Dr. Whaley's constant summer employment, the sale of my cattle and their calves, and the free room and board from Uncle Leon, I had been lucky to have obtained my university education.

For the first time in my life I felt that I was now completely in charge of my future. College had been a struggle and I was now deep in debt, but the prospect of what was to come next was intoxicating.

Now all I needed was a job!

A family photograph
Left to right, back row; Walter Alderman, Eunice Alderman, Bill Allen.
Front row; Jo Marie Alderman, Sandra Denise Alderman, David Lee
(Mike) Alderman at Uncle Charles King's house. Those in the photo were
facing into a strong setting sun. Christmas, 1959.

CHAPTER TWENTY-EIGHT

SARASOTA: A TIME TO TEACH

Between carrying seven courses and working at the Division of Plant Industry, I had neglected to start searching for a job in the spring of 1961. I failed to realize that finding a professional position took time. Now that I was the first university graduate in the Allen family, I was feeling pressure to be employed. I stayed on in the apartment with Elmer and Martha and worked full time for Wally Dekle. Every day at lunch, I checked in with Student Placement Services and filled out applications. I received no responses to my inquiries. By the middle of June, Wally's project was complete and so was my employment.

I told Elmer that I was heading back to Kissimmee. Temporarily, I moved in with Uncle Leon and continued to send out applications that the placement office had given me. I had left my Kissimmee address and phone number with the placement service in the hope that they would continue to help me find employment.

To make matters worse, my black and white 1951 Ford died a few days after I arrived back at home. I had bought the car from my brother Leon for $150 when he went to Viet Nam in 1959. I thought that it was a step up from the 1931 Chevy, but Uncle Leon said that he was not convinced. It mattered not, because Leon needed to sell it and he made the price right. I sold the 31 Chevy for thirty-five dollars, took my summer savings and paid cash. The kid that I sold it to wrecked the old Chevy one week later.

Students in their junior year were allowed to have cars and

I needed one to go back and forth to school. Davis had graduated, and I no longer had a ride to the university. The Ford had served its purpose, but now the cost estimate to repair it was beyond my ability to pay.

My feeling of desperation was growing stronger. For the first time, I could tell that Uncle Leon was uneasy with my return. He had taken me in at fourteen years old, fed me, provided shelter and served as a strong moral compass as I grew to be an adult. He felt that it was time for me to move on and I sensed it.

Four days after I returned, I got a phone call inquiring if I was interested in interviewing for a job teaching Vocational Agriculture at Sarasota High School. I was somewhat surprised because when I changed majors from Agricultural Education to Entomology, I had not taken practice teaching. It was a senior year required course.

I said yes and went downtown to check the bus schedules. The interview was to be two days later at two PM. The repair of my Ford automobile would have to wait until I made some money. To my surprise, there was no bus to Sarasota scheduled on the day of my interview. After reviewing the bus schedule, I found that there was a bus to Saint Petersburg on that date.

A good friend from college, Dave Smith, had returned to Largo after graduation, and was working on his father's egg farm. A horticulture graduate, he was planning to start an ornamental plant nursery. I called him and told him of my dilemma. He volunteered to drive me the forty miles to my interview and return me to the bus station for my trip home.

In college, I had ridden many times in his red and white MG convertible, but the drive over the Sunshine Skyway Bridge was breathtaking. I had never seen any place so beautiful. Vast expanses of clear, blue water in Tampa Bay flowed seamlessly into the Gulf of Mexico. Mangroves ringed the south end of the watery expanse. Sea gulls swooped down over the water and with my head above the top of the windshield, the fifty mile an hour breeze felt wonderful. The MG was not made for a person that was six feet, five inches tall. I knew in that moment that the west coast of Florida was where I wanted to be.

When I got to the interview, Dave parked under a tree and waited outside. At the conclusion of the committee's questions, the chairman asked me to wait outside of the interview room, and a few minutes later invited me back into the room. To my surprise, they offered me the job before I left the building. I immediately accepted. They then asked when I could start work and were pleased that I said July first. I was anxious to start earning some money.

They had me sign several papers and gave me some more papers to fill out and mail back after I returned to Kissimmee. The job paid $4,800 for a twelve month, provisional teaching appointment. Most teachers had nine month appointments that paid $3,600. I could not imagine having that much money.

On the bus trip home, I marveled about my sudden good fortune. In the course of a few days, I had gone from being almost indigent to having a secure job with a good salary.

On Friday, the last day of June, I went to Sarasota by bus, and took a taxi over to the school. It was about 2 p.m. when I checked in and signed a few more papers. There were only a couple of teachers around and a small number of administrative staff. School would not start until after Labor Day. Most teachers were employed for nine months and would report for duty on September first. Vocational Agriculture teachers were given twelve month employment so that they could follow up on their student's summer home projects. Without a car, I had to put home visits on hold for a while. The school did have a flat-bed truck assigned to the Vo-Ag department but it was not available for personal transportation. Summer home visits were considered personal transportation.

I inquired about finding an apartment. A secretary told me

that an English teacher, Miss Etta Scarborough, rented rooms to young teachers. I got her phone number and called about availability. It was about a mile from the school, so I could walk to the school until I solved the transportation problem. I left my suitcase at the school and walked to her house and upon inspection, rented one of the two available rooms for ten dollars a week. It had kitchen privileges but quiet hours were strictly adhered to. Etta was unmarried, but had her bed-ridden mother living with her. It was her mother who needed the quiet.

July first was a Saturday, so my first day at school was Monday, July 3, 1961. After a chat with the principal, I began my assignment by taking inventory of my new domain. I got a list of the students that were scheduled to be enrolled that year. They ranged from eighth graders to seniors. I would try to get familiar with their names. The classroom was in a large building behind the school. One half of the building housed the Auto Mechanics program and the other half was mine. A small assortment of hand tools, including a hammer and fence staples, were a part of the inventory but there were no books, pamphlets or visual aids. I asked about a slide projector, and was told that one would be supplied upon request when classes started.

The head secretary filled me in on some of the everyday responsibilities and in the process revealed that my budget would be 240 dollars. The budget was for the farm. "What farm?" I asked. The school was in the city with no farm land nearby. No one had mentioned this in the interview. I stopped by the principal's office and asked about the farm. He said that was indeed part of the job and that he would show me the property later that day.

The Vo-Ag farm was four miles from the school, in Fruitville. When we arrived, I opened the farm gate and noticed that it needed repair. The farm was about thirty acres of over-grazed, Bahia grass pastureland on a deep sandy soil.

Twenty head of undernourished cows and calves roamed about looking for something to eat. At one end of the property was a shallow drainage ditch that flowed from the adjacent housing development. It provided standing water for the cattle. A two acre swamp was on the edge of the property. Looking around I could see that the fence was in bad shape and realized that 240 dollars was not nearly enough to take care of this farm.

"It's not much of a farm. The boys like to come out here to see the cattle, but lately the cows have been getting out and bothering the neighbors. I hope that you can do something about that."

I listened to the principal in silence, but I completely agreed with his first statement.

As I walked home from school, I pondered all that I had learned that first day. The job was a big responsibility, there was hardly anything to work with, and because I had never participated in the practice teaching experience, I was totally unprepared for what lay ahead. I had never made a lesson plan, prepared a test, or taught a class. There were no teaching aids or a standardized curriculum. There was only an under-fed herd of cattle that had become a problem for the principal and the school board. It was time to lace up my boots and forge ahead. I had dealt with worse problems in my twenty-one years.

On the fifth of July, things did in fact get worse. The District VO-AG Director called to inform me that I was expected to attend the State Vocational Agriculture Teachers meeting in Daytona Beach in the first week in August. No expenses were offered, and I was still short of cash and without a car.

I called a friend from CLO who lived in Daytona Beach and inquired about cheap hotels near the meeting hotel. Upon hearing my predicament, he told me that they lived nearby and invited me to stay with him at his mother's house.

Once again someone had offered help when I needed it.

WILLIAM A. ALLEN

The following Saturday morning I got a phone call from the principal saying that some of the cows had broken the fence and were in the adjacent subdivision. I told him that I would put them back in, and fix the fence, but that I needed to use the truck. He agreed.

With the help of a few neighbors, the three cows and a calf were soon back in the pasture. I retrieved the hammer, staples and a partial roll of barbed wire from the truck and mended the fence. The neighbors were civil, but let me know that no one had done anything about this problem for a long time. I told them that I was new, but promised to try to find a solution.

I called Ken Clarke, the Extension Agent, introduced myself and explained my problem: too many cattle, too little grass and not enough money to replace the fence. With no cow pens and no loading chute, I had no way to turn the surplus cattle into the needed cash to repair the fence. He listened carefully, asked a few questions and then said that he would try to help. He called back in a couple of days, and told me to meet him and some cattlemen at the farm a few days later.

When I arrived, Ken introduced me to three men and after a few minutes of laying our plans, we started working. Ken, having other business to take care of, then left with my thanks. The first task was to dig a slanted hole in the ground and to pile up the excavated sand to make a mound at the back of the hole. Once the slanted hole was completed, we stomped down the sand mound to firm it up. One of the two cattle trucks the men had brought was backed in into the hole and the horse was unloaded. Uncle Leon had used this type of pit to unload his horse for many years.

The rider then mounted his horse and began looking over the herd for cattle and calves that he thought were in good enough condition to market. The choice of which animal to select was entirely his. He then roped it and drug it near the truck, where we took the rope from him and pulled, pushed and sometimes lifted the animal into the truck. When we finished, five animals had been loaded and were taken to the cattle market. There was no charge for their services. The money was deposited with the school and I now had enough money to run the program. I never asked for anyone's permission to sell the cattle although the cattle were property of the school board.

By the third week in July, I received a check from Uncle Leon for my last cow. He had sold the other cow and her calf, during my last year of college. He also knew that I needed the money to get a start in the new job. I was now officially out of the cattle business. And I had money to buy a used car. Uncle Leon had my 1951 Ford hauled away, presumably to a junk yard.

I wasted no time finding a red and white, 1956 Buick Century. It was the same model car that Dr. Whaley had owned, and it was my first car without major problems. I loved it from the time that I first saw it on the car lot. And now it was mine.

In August, I attended the State Vocational Agricultural Teachers meeting in Daytona Beach. I now had enough money for a room at the hotel but decided to accept my friend's offer of a place to stay. I arrived on Sunday and met his large Italian family. Sunday dinner was a special occasion with his mother cooking roasted garlic chicken and all the trimmings. Conversations were loud and animated, and there was a lot of laughing. I spent four nights on their couch and felt very welcome. They were warm and generous, and it was a great experience. The meeting was a bore.

Etta Scarborough was the first teacher to warn me that I would have students that were discipline problems. It was confirmed by the auto mechanics teacher who shared the other side of the building. It had long been school practice to send many of these students to our two classes.

"Most of them are really good kids but about twenty

percent will cause problems," he said. "The last teacher really had problems. You know how your office door opens out into the classroom? Some of the kids would wait until he was inside with the door shut and then they would quietly move the teacher's desk in front of the door so he could not get out. They would stack chairs and stuff on top of the desk to weigh it down. When he couldn't push it open, he would bang on the wall on my side and I'd have to come let him out. It happened more than once. None of the other kids would rat them out, so they never did get punished." Being forewarned, I asked the principal to have the door to my office reversed so that it opened inward, and I never had that problem.

When the students arrived that year, I soon realized that the lack of teaching aides and a standard curriculum was a problem. My personal textbooks had been sold when I left the university to get cash. I was not a polished classroom teacher and was winging it based on what I could remember from my university classes and practical experience. To compensate, I took the students to the farm for practical hands-on lessons.

I transported my students to the farm in the back of the school truck, two to three times a week. They learned to mend and replace fence, and we also built a primitive holding pen and a wooden loading chute. I talked about the breeds of cattle while pointing out the poor quality of the bull that we had. They were learning by doing, and the cows never again escaped into the subdivision. The principal seemed pleased.

Having success in the fencing project I thought that I should start another project. I realized that most of the kids in the program had never had a garden and I began to make plans to rectify that deficiency. The major problem would be water for the garden.

I selected a spot on the farm that seemed to be the best place for a garden, and had one of the students take a soil test to the county agent's office. It was about forty yards from the ditch with the water. I reasoned that if we could get a pump, that we could get water from the ditch to irrigate the garden. But where would we get a pump? The Auto Mechanics teacher suggested calling the Army-Navy Surplus Warehouse in Starke. He had bought from them, and schools were given rock bottom prices.

After contacting them, they told me that they could provide me with a pump at a good price. They told me to bring a trailer because it was heavy. I let him know that I would have to wait until the Thanksgiving break to pick it up. While waiting, I selected four teams of students to prepare for the pump's arrival. One team built a fence around the proposed garden spot. Another team built a covered platform for the pump to rest on, while a third team cut saplings from the little swamp and built a three-foot high log, brush, and earthen dam in the drainage ditch. The fourth team laid the decommissioned water pipe that I had been given by the water department. The pipe had holes in it, but I thought that the escaping water would irrigate the pasture between the pump and the garden.

On the Monday after Thanksgiving, I pulled the trailer containing the pump up close to the platform. With several of the stronger boys helping, we loaded it onto the platform. The pipes to the garden area and the intake pipe were then attached. We would let the senior boys, who had served as team captains, start it up the next day.

On the next day, I stopped at a small store on the way to the farm, to let everyone buy a soft drink to drink as part of a christening ceremony. Each boy had been allowed to choose his team and the team captain was chosen by the team members. They all were proud of what they had accomplished. After thanking the boys for their good work, it was time to crank the pump. A senior, Ronnie Card, was selected to start the engine and after a few pulls, the engine sprang into life. Water spouts formed where there were holes in the pipe and spread over the nearby pasture, and flooded the fenced garden spot.

Then our bubble burst. Within five minutes of starting, we had sucked almost all of the water from the 100 yard long drainage ditch. I shut the motor off and we stood there looking at the nearly-dry ditch in disbelief. Finally one of the boys started laughing and everyone joined in. It had been a spectacular failure. We never tried to start the pump again and we had no garden to show for our efforts. The only thing that we had gained was the students experience with team building.

CHAPTER TWENTY-NINE

DOROTHY LANGELAND: THE GIRL IN THE POODLE SKIRT

Between Thanksgiving and Christmas, I realized that I was probably not cut out to be a high school teacher. I felt good about giving my students practical experience, but my classroom performance was sub-par. Some people are not meant to work in this essential field, and I realized that I was one of them. I began to think about what I would do after the school year was over. Fortunately, someone else was thinking of my future too.

Dr. Milledge Murphey, the apiculture professor at the University of Florida, sent me a letter with a notice for a graduate assistantship at Purdue University. Jim Brogdon, an Extension Entomologist, had received it and passed it on to Milledge, with the notation that I might be interested. In my senior year, I had told Professor Brogdon that I thought that Extension was a field that I would like to pursue. I called and thanked both of them for thinking of me. That night I filled out the application, attached the requested supporting information, and mailed it the next day.

On New Year's Eve, 1961, I finally met the girl in the poodle skirt who was still listening to Pat Boone. While hauling chairs for the judges' platform for the New Year's Day Youth Rodeo, my ulcer began bothering me. I stopped at the Maas Brothers Lunch Counter to get a glass of milk, hoping that it might settle the burning in my stomach. At the counter across from me sat the most beautiful girl that I had ever seen. Nineteen year old

Dorothy Langeland was six feet tall, slender, with long blond hair, blue eyes and a nice smile.

Dorothy had recently moved to Florida from upstate New York, and was living with her grandfather, George (Gunwald) Langeland. She had completed her freshman year at Cedar Crest College in Allentown, Pennsylvania, but now needed to establish residency for one year, and earn money to enroll at the University of Florida.

She had been hired by the department store to sell handbags during the lead up to Christmas. She and other seasonal employees had been let go because Christmas was over. Dorothy had not seen it coming and was irritated. I watched her as I drank my milk. She was trying to get the waitress to refill her tea cup, but was not having much luck. I had very little experience with girls in my life, but decided to introduce myself by telling the waitress to give her another teabag.

Over tea and milk we talked for about twenty minutes before I asked her for a date. At first she said no, that she did not know me. I persisted by telling her that she never would if her answer was still no. After a few minutes she accepted my invitation.

As it turned out, she only lived three blocks from where I did. When I arrived to pick her up, her grandfather told me that she had gone out with her girlfriends. I had been stood up and was disappointed. As it turned out, she had been given some incorrect information from a friend at Maas Brothers.

The previous October, a senior girl from the neighborhood had showed up at the house where I was living and asked for a ride to school. She said that she had missed the bus. I accommodated her and thought nothing of it. A few days later, the same thing happened again. After several such incidences, Miss Scarborough, my landlady and fellow teacher, recognized a problem that I had been oblivious to. She warned me to put an end to it. I had not realized that the girl had a crush on me.

Miss Scarborough and I talked about the problem and she suggested that I tell the student that I was married, but my wife could not be with me until a later date. I did so, and the student never missed the bus again. Having taught for nearly thirty five years, Miss Scarborough had seen it all before. I did not have a clue.

Dorothy's friend relayed this misinformation to Dorothy, and it almost ended our relationship before it even started.

The next week, as I was leaving school, I heard someone calling my name in the parking lot. I looked up and there Dorothy was in one of her girlfriend's convertible car. She had found out that the story was not true, and came to apologize. I believed her, accepted her apology and asked her out again. We started seeing one another almost daily after that. In three week's time, I had developed strong feelings for her, and knew that she was the girl that I had always hoped to find.

I received a letter of acceptance to attend Purdue shortly after New Year's Day 1962.

In late January, Dorothy invited me to her parent's home in Port Charlotte. Her mother, Virginia, and father, Arthur, had recently moved there from Pound Ridge, New York. Virginia had been a nurse and Arthur was a carpenter. Port Charlotte was a backwater town in 1962. It was just getting off the drawing board with a few hundred homes and a strip mall. Neither of them had found work at wages that were acceptable.

Virginia hugged me when I first came in the door. She was warm and welcoming and bubbling with energy, and I liked her immediately. Arthur was more reserved. Her fourteen year old brother, Ken, was enrolled in school in Punta Gorda. Ken was a kid that liked the outdoors and was adjusting to his new life in the south, but he missed the deep forests around Pound Ridge. Ken, his neighborhood friend Herbie, and Ken's dog Shep, were exploring the adjacent piney woods and finding that there was a lot to like about the new landscape. I liked Ken right away.

Their small house was constructed of concrete block, with terrazzo floors. As was common in those days, it also had no air conditioning. Living as I had all my life, I thought it was elegant.

By February, I realized that I was in love with Dorothy and decided to take her home to Kissimmee, so that she could meet my relatives. That was going to be complete culture shock, but before our relationship went any further, I thought that she should meet them. I chose the weekend of the Silver Spurs Rodeo.

I gave her some warning about what to expect. She had heard about some of my background, but thought that I was exaggerating. We left after school on Friday and did not arrive at Uncle Leon's house until nine PM. I had called ahead to let Uncle Leon and Aunt Sabra know that we were coming. I told Dorothy that when we drove up, Uncle Leon might meet us with a flash light and a shotgun, which he did. Dorothy was surprised, but remained fearless. It being late we all turned in. He and Aunt Sabra had been in bed when we arrived, perhaps thinking that we were not coming this late. To our surprise, they gave Dorothy their bed, and moved to the bed that I had always slept on. Her bed was already warmed up! I slept on the couch.

The next morning, Uncle Leon took Dorothy and me to see his cattle which were pastured near the house. He had a purebred Brahma bull that was extremely gentle, and Dorothy delighted in scratching its neck. The bull liked it too. Later that day we took in the rodeo. Dorothy loved all of the horse events, especially the barrel racing and the rider's quadrille. It had been a good day.

Dorothy Langeland scratching the dewlap on Uncle Leon's
Brahma bull. Uncle Leon is in the picture.

After supper, I drove downtown to show Dorothy the night
lights of the sleepy little town of Kissimmee. When we returned
home that night, I stopped the car on the cattle guard about a
hundred yards from the house, and proposed marriage. To my
delight, she said yes, but asked me to not announce it until she
could tell her mother.

It was hard not telling anyone about my good news. We
planned to visit Mom on Sunday morning, and I knew that she
would be curious about why I had brought this beautiful young
girl with me. I needed to be evasive.

Mom and Walter were now renting a small house off
Vineland Road, on the banks of Shingle Creek. Across the creek
and about a hundred yards north was a log cabin where Dad's
older brother, Cliff, had once lived with his wife, Flossie, and
their children. My cousin Henry and I had spent many happy

hours fishing on the banks of Shingle Creek.

When we arrived, Mom came out to meet us at the car. They had no phone, and she had not known that we were in town. When she came close, we noticed that she had a black eye. Fearing the worst, I asked about it, and she told me that Alice Yowell had accused Walter of being a hog thief, and she had taken exception. It was not clear how Alice made out, but Mom had a real shiner. That was Dorothy's introduction to her prospective mother-in-law.

Mom invited us in, where Dorothy met Denise, Jo Marie, Mike and Walter. David's name had been changed to Mike after Walter married Mom. Dorothy was getting a complete picture of my family, and I wondered whether or not she was reconsidering her decision. She had been forewarned, but probably was a little stunned. After our visit with Mom, we returned to Sarasota and Dorothy called her mother. We had known each other only six weeks and I am sure her mother was shocked.

Newly engaged, I needed a ring for Dorothy. Once again I was almost broke. With the money I made from the sale of my last cow, I had bought an automobile, but was still making payments. Even though I had kitchen privileges, I had limited culinary talents, and ate most of my meals in commercial kitchens. My first few paychecks had gone for living expenses, and purchasing a better wardrobe. Jeans and tee shirts had been fine for a student, but more was expected from a teacher.

Not wanting to spend Christmas with Etta Scarborough and her dying mother, I had returned two months earlier to Kissimmee on Christmas Eve 1961 for a three day visit with my relatives. Realizing that Mom was short of cash and struggling, I wrote her a check for most of what I had saved.

Dorothy was aware of my financial situation. We shopped for a ring together and selected one that I could afford. The ring set cost $127. The diamond was tiny. She still wears it after fifty seven years.

Almost all of our dates consisted of dancing at the Landmark Hotel on Lido Beach. The Landmark was a luxury hotel, with most of the clientele being retired people on their Florida vacation. We were usually the only ones less than forty five years old. The new dance was the twist, and the sight of a tall, beautiful blond in a micro- miniskirt on the dance floor was enough to often make the band put the spotlight on her. She never liked the attention, but we both liked to dance. Customers tried to buy us drinks, but she was under age and I had an ulcer. Later we would walk on the beach in the moonlight, and share a piece of pie and coffee at the Dutch Pantry.

We married June 17, 1962, and left for Purdue University pulling a U-Haul trailer, filled with assorted used furniture that neighbors had given us, and less than three hundred dollars. She was 19 and I was 22 years old. Our first night we stopped at a cheap motel in Tarpon Springs which was across from the waterfront. The second day we stopped too often, and drove too late, that the only room that we could find was at a truck stop in Dothan, Alabama. By the third day, we were traveling the back roads of Kentucky and found a four dollar a night log cabin surrounded by deep forests. We completed our journey to Lafayette, Indiana, on the fourth day, and checked into a "Mom and Pop Motel" on the edge of town. We were tired of driving, and ready to be settled down in a place of our own.

The next morning, we checked into our apartment at the Married Student Courts, went downtown and bought a bed for same-day delivery, then unloaded and returned the trailer. The two-room apartment was located near one edge of the campus and was within easy walking distance of the entomology building. Each of the twenty or so brick buildings in Married Student Courts was composed of eight apartments, and the population of students and their children was high. On campus the apartments were referred to as "Fertile Valley" or "Rabbit Row." Children were everywhere.

I went to work the next morning. There had been no honeymoon trip, but we, at last, were settled in and beginning married life. In the years ahead we would travel extensively. Each time, Dorothy would say that it was our lost honeymoon and we would laugh.

CHAPTER THIRTY

LEARNING EXTENSION WORK; PURDUE AND PINELLAS COUNTY

Dorothy and I spent two years at Purdue, while I completed the requirements for a Master's Degree in Entomology. To earn my $220 per month assistantship, I worked twenty hours a week, identifying insects and responding to Extension Agent requests for information on insect control. In the summer, I traveled to County Fairs to judge honey and 4-H insect exhibits. Traveling the back roads of Indiana, I was astounded by the vastness of mid-west agriculture. Nothing had prepared me for the large fields of corn, soybeans and small grains, or the number of hog farms that covered the landscape. I quickly learned that farmers and Extension Agents appreciated my help, and I knew that I had made the right career change. Extension Entomology would be my life's work. Most important of all, I was learning from a wonderful Major Professor, Glen Lehker.

Professor Lehker, and another Extension Entomologist, Dave Mathews, gave me a chance to be heavily involved in the everyday duties of Extension Entomology. Unlike most of the graduate students who had their desk in a large room with other students, I had an office adjacent to Glen and Dave. This arrangement gave me an opportunity to constantly interact with them. It was a good working arrangement as both men took an interest in the practical aspects of my education. In addition to the previously mentioned duties, I took phone calls from agents, wrote extension pamphlets and helped with training sessions for agents and farmers. They exposed me to every facet of my future career.

Professor Lehker was well respected in the field, and took me under his wing, teaching me how Extension work should be conducted. He was a master at speaking and simultaneously drawing cartoon illustrations with chalk. His chalk-talks were widely requested. It did not take long to realize how fortunate I was to have him as my Major Professor.

He was very organized and direct in his mentorship. He expected the same of me and the Extension Agents that we served. I had been there only about three weeks when he called me into his office, and told me to take a seat. After closing the door he got right to the point. "Allen, if you want to make a living in Extension, you need to learn to speak so that other people can understand you." I was shocked by the directness of his words. "Learn to speak like the people you hear on TV, and here in Indiana. They all speak with a mid-west accent that is recognized all across the country," he added.

I felt somewhat humiliated and took the afternoon off to think over his admonition. I had not realized that my strong southern accent and poor grammar was so alien in the north. Finally I came to the conclusion that he would not have said something so personal, unless it was important. I had come for an education, and even though the first lesson was humbling, I started listening to how others spoke. Over time, I lost most of my accent. It had been a tough lesson but an important one.

Realizing that I needed a different curriculum of study for an Extension career, he suggested a master's thesis topic that was controversial for the Department of Entomology. Instead of researching the biology and/or control of an insect, we chose to evaluate extension methods in twelve mid-western states. The research consisted of surveying nearly a thousand Extension Agents in the twelve states about what they wanted from Extension Entomologists, and comparing the results to the programs being provided by their Entomology Departments.

When the work was finished I reported the findings at the national Entomological Society of America meetings in St. Louis in December 1963. It was the first professional Entomology meeting that I attended. I was given thirty minutes in a Plenary Session for my report, and at the time had no idea that most speakers only got ten minutes to report their work. It would be years before I got that much time again. Professor Lehker and I both felt good about my research, because several states used our findings to make major modifications to their programs the following year.

In the course of the four day meeting, I took in scientific papers and listened in rapt attention as the President of that large, august body of scientists gave his Presidential address. Sitting there among the huge throng of scientists, I imagined that I might someday become President, and decided that I would make it a career goal. Perhaps it was only a dream, but I was too young and inexperienced to know that.

While at Purdue, I made a second goal that was difficult to imagine as young as I was. The Extension Director, Dr. Howard Dieselin, had his office in the building adjacent to ours. As part of my training, Professor Lehker required me to attend open Extension Faculty meetings with him when classes allowed. I was the only graduate student in attendance, and the Director sometimes talked with me about my future career. I decided then that I wanted to be an Extension Director some day. Both goals were ambitious to the point of being folly.

While I was studying and working, Dorothy took a position in the main administration building. Her unit handled the mail and sent out university checks. Our joint income greatly improved our quality of life and in May of 1963, Dorothy pointed out that May was National Baby Month. I assured her that I would do my part, and we started planning to expand our family. Dorothy worked until a short time before our first child, Morgan, was born on February 1, 1964.

On August 10, 1964, having completed the degree

requirements for a master's degree, I reported for a job as Agricultural Extension Agent in Pinellas County, Florida. I was one of seven agents in the office and my area of work was to be horticulture. I had not finished my research in time for June graduation, but had my diploma mailed to me in December.

Pinellas County comprises an area from St. Petersburg to Tarpon Springs and all the municipalities in between. It was there that I would learn how Extension works at the county level. The jobs were very different. The county position was broader in scope and required a greater commitment of time than what I had observed in the Extension Entomology role at the state level. State level positions required a deeper knowledge of subject matter and a great deal more travel.

During a brief chat with Gil Whitton, the Unit Director, I learned that my area of responsibility would be extensive. I would serve the commercial and residential horticultural needs of the county. Specific duties included: providing educational programs for 400,000 home owners, 600 people that held a nursery license, farmers with 1600 acres of citrus and an estimated 2000 lawn maintenance people. My media duties included a daily radio program, three articles a week for the St. Petersburg Times and the Clearwater Sun newspapers and a weekly 30 minute television program that I shared with Gil. I had inherited this program from Gil, when he was moved up to the Unit Director position. Our public media work was presented under the monikers of "The Old Dirt Dauber" (Gil) and "The Green Giant." It was the first time that I had been given a radio program or a TV program and there was a big learning curve. Fortunately, Gil was a good reference on almost anything that I encountered, and there was an extensive film and document collection from which to learn.

Bill Allen helping an unidentified homeowner with a
plant problem, circa 1965.

Bill Allen "the Green Giant" with his weekly television show
"Growing Things", circa 1967

Three nights a week and many of my lunch periods were spent speaking to civic clubs about home-owner related issues. A Home Demonstration Extension Agent, Dorothy Draves, and I taught a two hour class for those who cared to attend our classes in St. Petersburg, Largo and Tarpon Springs, on Monday, Wednesday and Friday mornings respectively.

The Pinellas Chapter of the Florida Nursery and Growers Association was a special group of clientele. They held monthly meetings at the auditorium attached to our offices and were major supporters of our program. Each year I served on the Agricultural Fair Board and was tasked with filling the huge building reserved for horticulture. The nurserymen all chipped in to fill the building. There were at least a hundred thousand dollars worth of fountains, stone work, orchids, trees, and other plants on display. It was always the most visited building at the fair.

My work with the horticulture industry was very fulfilling

professionally and socially. I made friends with many of them and tried to serve everyone who had a production problem, often calling in extension specialists from the University of Florida to solve their most serious problems. In gratitude and friendship the Pagano Brother's Nursery in Pinellas Park, surprised me one day by naming one of their new hybrid hibiscus varieties "The Bill Allen". It was totally unexpected but I could not have been more pleased.

Meanwhile, Dorothy was holding down the home front and bringing into our lives another son, Erik Leon, on February 28, 1966. In the same year that we celebrated Erik's arrival, we mourned Uncle Leon's death on December 18. He was laid to rest south of Kissimmee in Pleasant Hill Cemetery, a place that housed the remains of many early settler families, The land for the cemetery had been donated by my great grandparents Steve Acree and Eliza Lanier Acree. Steve and Eliza, and two of Eliza's sons, John and James, and many of our family are buried there. Aunt Sabra arranged to have his gravestone reflect the life that he lived. He was a working cattleman with few peers.

Leon Vernon Allen's gravestone depicting his life as a cattleman.

As demanding as my schedule was, the years in Pinellas County were also hard for Dorothy. I often was not home for meals or to help put the children to bed. She listened to my daily radio broadcasts, while feeding our sons, and pointed out that it was my voice on the radio. She was afraid that they might forget it.

As difficult as her life was because of my schedule, Dorothy never complained. When we had time to go to the beach or out to dinner, it was special but even that was often interupted. With a large media and public speaking presence, many people recognized me when we were away from home, and would come over to our dinner table to discuss their problems. They had no way of knowing that our dinner at the Oyster Bar might be the only dinner that we ate by ourselves that week. We grew used to the interruptions and Dorothy was always gracious.

There was very little downtime in the four years that I was in that position. While there, I learned to manage time, programs and events. Dorothy learned to manage a household and two small boys with very little help. Eventually it was time to move on, and in the fall of 1967, I started applying for jobs to Entomology Departments that offered Ph.D. degrees. More education was the key to achieving my family's needs, and the professional goals that I had made at Purdue.

In the end of February 1968 I said good-bye to my television, radio and newspaper audiences, and to my co-workers and friends in Pinellas County. The job had allowed me to learn and grow professionally and I was now ready for a new start.

PART THREE

CLIMBING MOUNTAINS, NEW VISTAS
AND A PLACE CALLED HOME

CHAPTER THIRTY-ONE

THE RIGHT PLACE

I called the United States Department of Agriculture and talked to the Federal Extension Entomologist, Paul Bergman, to inquire about jobs that might be available across the country. I had met Paul while at Purdue and to my surprise he said that he had applied for an assistant position in Washington, DC. He was waiting approval of the position and would keep me in mind, if I was interested. I thanked him, but told him that I wanted to get a Ph.D. and needed a school that offered one. He then suggested that I get in touch with the University of Delaware who was looking for someone to fill an Extension Entomologist position. I called Dr. Dale Bray, the Department Head in Delaware, and applied a few days later.

I also got in touch with Dr. Bill Eden, Department Head at the University of Florida. After phone discussions and a visit to his office, Dr Eden told me that a faculty member was taking a leave of absence from his Extension Entomologist position to pursue a Ph.D. degree at Purdue University. Dr. Eden offered to have me transferred from my county responsibilities into the position while he was away. I could work on my degree while working full-time, but when I finished my degree, I would have to leave. It is accepted practice at most universities, that they do not hire their own graduates. I explained that I wanted to be eligible for employment at the University of Florida when I finished my education, and declined his offer. Dr. Eden said that he understood, reached into his desk and pulled out a flier from Virginia Polytechnic Institute. It was advertising an opening for a Survey Entomologist position. I applied for the position two days later.

I was offered both positions and accepted the VPI job with a starting date of March 1, 1968. We sold the house; put our possessions in storage and moved Dorothy and the boys in with her parents, who were now living in Sarasota. We had been promised an apartment but the previous occupants were unable to move out until the house that they were building was finished. I headed for Blacksburg and arrived in a blinding snowstorm. With no place to stay, I inquired about cheap motels and was told that they were full. Hearing of my plight, John Amos, the Extension Apiculturist, invited me stay with him and his wife Edna until the apartment came available. It was a generous offer and in the next three weeks we became fast friends.

Before Dorothy and the boys arrived, the moving company gave notice that they were delivering our household goods. I still had no apartment and could find no empty storage space to rent for just a week or two. The Department Head, Dr. Jim Grayson, who had twice invited me to dinner with his family, suggested that I use their stand-alone garage. His wife, Margaret, had located our apartment before we arrived and wanted to make sure that we were off to a good start in our new community. They were both special people and Dr. Grayson was an administrator revered by the faculty, staff and students, long after the twenty years he served as Department Head.

Three weeks after I arrived, the apartment became available. Dorothy, Morgan and Erik caught the next plane to Roanoke, where she took one look at the mountains, and declared that she was never leaving. She still had not seen Blacksburg, but was already in love with Virginia. Blacksburg turned out to be the cherry on top of the cake for both of us.

Finally in our apartment, I started surveying the state for crop damaging insects, and signed up for my first class. My annual salary of $11,000 was enough to take care of our family expenses. I also began classes part-time, but class time had to yield to employment responsibilities. From the third week in March, to the middle of October, I traveled two to three days almost every week searching for insect outbreaks. Sixteen hundred copies of my report were mailed to constituents each Friday at noon, for arrival in their Monday mail. It was a popular report started by Bill Isakson, the person who had held the job before me. Extension Agents depended on the report for early warning programs in their counties, and farmers wanted to be forewarned too.

The year 1968 turned out to be an explosive year for the nation. While I was settling in to my new job and community, Dr. Martin Luther King was leading the civil rights movement. He had gone to Memphis, Tennessee, to support the garbage workers, in their bid for higher wages and better working conditions. Racial tensions were high but King knew that his presence would be needed to support the garbage workers' requests. Having received death threats, he went anyway.

On my second survey trip in my new job, I was assessing alfalfa weevil damage to alfalfa in the central region of the state. I spent the third night of the trip in a small motel near the entrance to Appomattox Court House National Historical Park, with the intent to finish my report in the motel that night, briefly see the park the next morning, and return home. I awoke the next morning with the news that on the night before, Thursday, April 4, 1968, James Earl Ray had shot and killed Dr. King at the Lorraine Motel in Memphis. The nation was in mourning. The civil rights movement had lost its leader. Civil unrest would follow in the days ahead.

Two months later, Ray would be captured at Heathrow Airport in London, England, as he tried to flee the country. He was extradited back to the US for trial. Ray confessed to the crime, was convicted on his 41st birthday and imprisoned for the rest of his life. He died on April 23, 1998, in Nashville, Tennessee, of natural causes.

Later that summer a similar fate befell Senator Bobby Kennedy who was running for the Democratic nomination for President. Kennedy was shot by Sirhan Sirhan shortly after midnight on June 5, while leaving through the kitchen of the Ambassador Hotel in Los Angeles, California. He died 26 hours later on June 6, 1968. The evening before he was shot, Kennedy had learned the he had won the California and Idaho primaries. His death prompted the United States Secret Service to begin protecting presidential candidates. The nation was once again in shock.

On August 26-28th the Democrats held their convention in Chicago, Illinois. Anti-war tensions were at a breaking point and street riots soon followed. It seemed like the whole nation was turning on itself, and that we could find no answer to the hate and division.

Back in Blacksburg, Virginia, the lease on the apartment ran out at the end of August, 1968. Margaret Grayson again found us a place to rent; a house on the corner of Washington Street and Water Street (now Draper Road). There was a housing shortage in the small town of Blacksburg. Margaret was well connected in the community, and with the university growing rapidly, under the leadership of President Dr. Marshal Hahn, rental properties were more often handled by word of mouth than by realtors.

The house was perfectly located between the university and the town. It had plenty of living space, and there were fruit trees, grape vines and a large garden plot. Our sons had a small barn to play in, and boys their age lived nearby. I could walk to work, pick up Morgan and Erik from Methodist Kindergarten, and be home for lunch with the family. Dorothy had a Red Flyer wooden wagon that she used to transport our sons to stores downtown. Every store that we needed was within seven blocks of our house.

VPI had a large Cadet Corp and the Cadet Marching Band often would march down Washington Street playing Sousa

Marches and school fight songs at dinner time. When the boys would hear the band coming, they left the table and ran with our collie, Rusty, to the fence surrounding our yard as the parade went by. We all learned to be inspired by the band's performance.

Parades, with all the floats, cadets, cheerleaders, fraternities and sororities marched by on Homecoming Weekend, providing a show for the whole family. Sporting events provided a steady stream of students and alumni hurrying by on their way to the game, and many stopped long enough to give Rusty a pat on the head. When Morgan and Erik were not entertaining Rusty, the dog spent much of her time near the fence, knowing that students often shared part of whatever they were eating with her.

By June 1968, my Major Professor, Dr. Bob Pienkowski, and I selected a research project for my Ph.D. dissertation. The Frit Fly, <u>Oscinella</u> <u>frit</u>, an insect the size of an eye gnat, was damaging reed canary grass in Dr. Dale Wolf's Agronomy research plots. Little was known about this species in North America, although it was considered to be a pest of small grains in Northern Europe and Russia. I decided to work out the insect's biology and create a life table, calculating mortality rates at each stage of the insect's development. Only one life table of an insect had ever been reported in entomological literature and that had been completed by several Canadian scientists working on a much larger insect species, the Spruce Budworm. My choice for a research project was an ambitious undertaking.

Field samples for my dissertation research were collected on Friday afternoons after I finished my weekly survey work. Sunday mornings were reserved for processing the samples that I had collected on Friday. Much of the work took place in a room above the garage at our home using a microscope that I borrowed from the department. This allowed the boys to see more of me, and I of them.

Saturdays were family days and we sometimes took the boys to the university's sheep barn to let them play with the kittens that always seemed to be in the hay barn. When time permitted, I played softball and basketball with the department teams, and Dorothy brought the boys to watch. On Sunday afternoons we went for drives to get ice cream. Blacksburg was an idyllic little town for young families.

Christmas vacations were always spent with Dorothy's parents in Sarasota. We all loved leaving the cold to go to the beach for a mid-winter excursion.

Like millions of people around the world, we watched the moon landing on July 20, 1969, from the living room of the house on Washington Street. We let Morgan and Erik stay up past their bedtime so that they might be a part of that historic moment. Morgan was five years old and Erik was three. They may have been too young to appreciate what was happening, but I wanted them to be a part of it. On May 25, 1961, President Kennedy had pledged the nation to send men to the moon and return them safely home by the end of the decade. Neil Armstrong, Buzz Aldrin, and Michael Collins had accomplished the mission with the whole world watching. Americans everywhere put aside their differences to cheer them on as the whole world watched the spectacle unfold on live television. We were all proud to be Americans.

Later that summer, we again watched on TV events that changed American culture. The war in Vietnam raged on with bitter divisions among Americans. Protests against the war were sweeping the nation and young men were burning their draft cards and women were burning their bras. On August 15-17, in Bethel and White Lake, New York, a music festival billed as "three days of peace and music" attracted 400,000 people to hear more than thirty acts, many performed in the rain. It would forever be remembered as "Woodstock."

We did not attend.

The years flew by as we watched Morgan and Erik grow up

and start school.

Dorothy held the family together, while I worked on my dissertation research, finished my class studies, and worked full time as Survey Entomologist. There was a lot of freedom in survey work and I enjoyed my time in Virginia's croplands. In the spring I concentrated on alfalfa and apples, then moved to corn, and soybeans as the seasons progressed.

During my travels, I began collecting insects that I could add to the reference collection and use in research studies. I later would publish papers on the Geographical and Seasonal Distribution of Tabanids (Horseflies and Deerflies) and on Pentatomids (Stink bugs).

When I had first arrived at VPI, I shared a small office with Bill Isakson, the previous Survey Entomologist. Bill had resigned from the job to finish writing his dissertation. He was helpful in orienting me to my new responsibilities and the crops and geography of Virginia.

I inherited a desk, a clipboard, one 18 x 24 lab table and a stereo-microscope with a lens that was so scratched that it was hard to see a hair taken from your arm. Two Cornell drawers housed the majority of the reference collection. There was no telephone at my desk, but one was available on Dr. John Weidhass's desk, on the other side of the wall. A hole had been cut in the wall and when I needed to use the phone, he would pass it through the opening. A university-owned car was provided and a travel budget was generous for the work to be performed.

Price Hall was crowded. The University was expanding rapidly and Price Hall housed several departments. Entomology shared the building with the Departments of Plant Pathology, Weed Science, Forestry, Fisheries, Wildlife and Biology. After Deering Hall was finished, Biology moved out and when the College of Forestry, Wildlife, and Fisheries was formed, they received a separate building. Departments were all in the same boat when it came to space, and no one had enough room for their programs in those first few years. Equipment, space and tasks were shared. Lifelong friendships were formed as everyone learned to share and to make do. There was no time or place for "Prima Donnas".

Dorothy and I had a tumultuous start in our new community, but we now were growing comfortable with our town, with the university and my job. We had found the right place. Blacksburg and VPI (soon to be Virginia Tech) were home.

CHAPTER THIRTY-TWO

INTEGRATED PEST MANAGEMENT

I earlier had decided to improve the insect reference collection during my first summer in 1968. Each week as I traveled the state I added pinned insect specimens to the Cornell drawers and began storing insect larvae in vials of alcohol. The insects were caught during the day, and I pinned and labeled them at night in my motel room. In midsummer, I requested that money be transferred from my travel budget to buy a new stereo microscope. My request was granted and insect identification took a great leap forward. Suddenly, I could see distinguishing features of the specimens to be identified.

The stereo microscope and reference collection were important to support Extension Agents. When faced with an insect problem that they did not recognize, they mailed specimens to me. In the fall of 1968, I developed forms and protocols for sending specimens and soon was able to efficiently process large numbers of insects. Those initial steps were the beginning of the Insect Identification Laboratory.

After the four departments of Biology, Fisheries, Wildlife, and Forestry moved out of Price Hall, the two remaining departments received the vacated space. Dr. Grayson, the Department Head, awarded me three rooms in the new space allocations. The rooms consisted of a large office for me, a spacious laboratory for the new Insect Identification Laboratory, and an office for the secretary and a new technician that I shared with John Weidhaas. The technician helped with the large volume of insect specimens that we were now receiving from Extension Agents. From that humble beginning the Insect Identification Laboratory has continued to grow and has become a large, highly-important program under the leadership of Erik Day.

In late summer 1971, Nick Ptucha, the Extension Agent for Westmoreland County, approached me as I was checking a soybean field for insect damage. He asked several questions about what I was finding and then asked the question that was really on his mind. "How do you know if a field needs spraying for insects?" He commented that he really had no answers for that decision and asked if I could help find one. Nick said that he suspected that a great many farmers were over-spraying. He then added that farmers often made their decision to spray when they saw the spray plane flying over a neighbor's field. He was suspicious that an unscrupulous spray plane operator might start a panic among farmers by simply spraying water over a field near a well traveled road. I had no answers for his questions, but told him that I would look in to it.

Rachel Carson had published her book "Silent Spring" on the first day of September, 1962, and the book had stirred an environmental awareness about the overuse of pesticides, particularly DDT. At first, the book was widely thought to be inaccurate and alarmist, but slowly people everywhere began to question the widespread use of agricultural pesticides. Nick's concern was appropriate and well founded. The need to know was both environmental and economic.

Soybean ecosystems are a complex mix of biology and cropping systems. Most fields in Virginia are small, by farming standards. They were usually less than twenty five acres, and were a part of a crop rotation regimen with corn, peanuts and small grains. Although the soybean crop-damaging insects were limited to Mexican bean beetles, corn earworm and stinkbugs, there are a large number of other insects in an unsprayed field. Many are predator insects and others may not cause enough damage to reduce yields. Once spraying began, the predator insects were killed and any subsequent infestation of economically important insects had no natural control.

It was common practice to spray early in the season to control the first generation of Mexican bean beetles. The beetles were the first to cause defoliation and reduce yields. Adult beetles overwintered in weeds and grasses near the fields and emerged from their winter hideouts to attack crops and lay eggs. Those eggs hatched into larvae that ate leaves and gave rise to an exponentially larger, second and third generation of beetles. Once spraying started, there were no predator insects to suppress the last two generations of beetles. Farmers were then on an insecticidal treadmill that would only get worse when the corn earworms arrived to eat the bean pods. Farmers were often spraying their fields three times in a season.

Knowing the difference between species was the first step to solving the problem. Using a series of line drawings, I began teaching Extension Agents to distinguish crop damaging insects in the early stage of their development. The other insects were to be discounted. That proved difficult because the green cloverworm is a leaf eating caterpillar and many farmers in Virginia had trouble distinguishing it from corn earworms. Fear of an uncontrolled outbreak that could destroy a crop was palpable when we began the program.

That summer I had been using a shake cloth to estimate insect population density. It was a technology that had been developed by two scientists in Arkansas and I found it useful in my work. But the question remained "How many insects must be present before the cost of spraying can be justified?" Searching the literature, I found preliminary answers for corn earworm and Mexican bean beetle infestations. I added this information to my initial insect drawings, along with instructions for making and using a shake cloth. We now had the beginning of an educational program.

Teaching farmers to use the program was slow. Using insect thresholds was a new concept, and they were often uncertain of their ability to identify insects, and to measure their density. It soon became clear, that I needed to find a way to help farmers with their decisions.

In the summer of 1972, I conducted an experiment in Middlesex County to determine if it was economically feasible to hire and train scouts to make decisions for participating farmers. The experiment was successful, so I repeated it the following summer in the City of Virginia Beach. Both locations were chosen to represent different farming situations. The second year confirmed the fact that scouting soybeans could be profitable.

The study also yielded information that confirmed Nick's worst suspicions. More than 87% of spraying for corn earworm in both locations had been unnecessary. With this information, I knew that we had to develop a program that would reduce pesticide loads in the nearly 400,000 acres of Virginia soybeans.

With the help of Agricultural Economists, I later published the results with Dr. Jim Roberts, in the October 1974 Journal of Economic Entomology. Jim had helped finance the experiment and sometimes helped with data collection. It was the first paper of its kind to be published in that journal. More importantly, it was the beginning of our Integrated Pest Management Program for Virginia soybeans.

In the summer of 1974, with the help of Nick Ptucha and a group of soybean farmers, we started the first commercial scouting program in Virginia. Our first scout was Lucy Dos Passos, daughter of the famous author, John Dos Passos. She turned out to be an excellent choice. Local farmers knew her, and she was meticulous in collecting data. After her initial summer program success, other scouts expanded the program into other counties over the next few years. Although successful, the scouting program was only a first step in the program that I was building. In the years that followed, I developed survey techniques to estimate the size of the corn earworm populations before they attacked the soybean crop. A series of corn surveys in July accurately predicted the size of the following generations that could attack the beans. This knowledge allowed farmers and farm supply stores time to prepare for the infestation.

Bill Allen training soybean scouts, circa 1975.

I next got our agents to change some of their farmers farming practices. By narrowing the distance between rows of soybeans, the canopy of the crop closed before the second generation of corn earworm moths emerged from nearby corn fields. This minimized the corn earworm moth's ability to penetrate the canopy and lay eggs on the bean pods. A second strategy to close the canopy was to get farmers to plant as early as possible. Farmers began to adopt both practices once they understood the significance of the changes. We were making progress with the corn earworm, but the Mexican bean beetle was still a major roadblock.

The final piece of the Mexican bean beetle puzzle was solved jointly with Dr. Pete Schultz, who worked for the Virginia Department of Agriculture and Consumer Services. Pete and I designed an experiment to use a newly introduced parasitic wasp, <u>Pediobius</u> <u>fovealatus</u>, to control the early field invasions of Mexican bean beetles. The wasp was a native of India and had been brought to this country by Dr. Reese Sailer of the USDA. It could not overwinter in cold climates but proved to be a major contributor in the quest to reduce pesticide use in the crop.

Each winter, Pete maintained a live colony of the wasps in a greenhouse at the Virginia Beach Research Station (now renamed the Virginia Tech Hampton Roads Agricultural Research and Extension Center). In the spring, I asked a number of farmers to plant plots of green beans near their soybean fields. The garden-sized plots were planted two weeks earlier than the adjacent soybean crop, to allow the green beans to emerge first. By emerging earlier, we could be sure that Mexican bean beetles that over-wintered nearby would find and colonize the plots of green beans. Once the beetles laid eggs on the green beans and the larvae hatched, Pete brought the parasitic wasps from the green house and introduced them into the plots.

When the tiny wasp laid an egg in the developing Mexican bean beetle larvae, the wasp's egg would divide into many dozens of wasp larvae and develop into a new generation of adult parasitic wasps. The reproductive potential of the wasp was already well known to Pete and me from his lab work. It completed a generation in a very short period of time. Upon emerging, the next batch of wasps was off in search of other Mexican bean beetle larvae. Having successfully launched the wasps, we needed to know how far the wasp would fly in search of new prey. Over the course of the summer my surveys documented a range of more than forty miles. It was far greater than we had dared to imagine. We immediately knew that this might be the turning point that we had been looking for.

As the summer progressed, the wasps that we released early in the season greatly reduced populations of the beetles. Many farmers no longer needed to make those early sprays that traditionally had started the chemical treadmill.

When Nick Ptucha had first asked for answers about spraying decisions, Virginia farmers were spraying most of its nearly 400,000 acres of soybeans two or three times each year. With the IPM program now turning the corner, I turned it over to Dr. Bob McPherson, and he in turn to Dr. Ames Herbert. Both of them were excellent young scientists that continued to lead, make changes and improve the program. In one later year, it was estimated that only 40,000 acres had been sprayed.

Along the way, graduate students had made contributions to the program at every step of program development. I had the pleasure of serving as the Major Professor for six graduate students, all of whom went on to become successful in life.

It had been a team effort and we were all pleased to have made a contribution to crop protection and a cleaner environment.

Those early efforts jump-started my career and led to opportunities that I, otherwise, would never have had. I was recognized by a great many organizations, including The Entomological Society of America and the American Soybean Association. Travel accompanied many of those opportunities, and I took Dorothy when it could be arranged.

CHAPTER THIRTY-THREE

GERMANY: THE FIRST TIME OVER THE POND

After five years of working and going to school, I received my Ph.D. in June 1973. It was a welcome relief. Sundays and evenings were suddenly free. I could now concentrate solely on my family and my work. I took pleasure in mowing the lawn at the house that we had bought the year before. Even so, there still was no time to relax. In one year's time I would stand for tenure and nothing was guaranteed.

A few months before I graduated, Dorothy, the kids and I went to Sarasota for an Easter vacation. We always brought our dog Rusty, so we really crowded Dorothy's parent's home anytime we came but Dorothy's extroverted mother, Virginia, always made us welcome. At Christmas we often stayed for two weeks. Virginia later told me that the reason the house always seemed so crowded was that the house was designed for two people in retirement, and was only nine hundred square feet. Fortunately there was a large lanai. Dorothy's dad, Arthur, was introverted and while we were in town, spent much time in the garage with his ham radio and a gallon of Gallo Port wine. I have often wondered why he put up with us.

On this particular trip, we added to the pandemonium by bringing special friends, Wayne and Kathy Surles. Kathy worked with me and had been the first technician to help develop the Insect Identification Laboratory. Raised in La Cross, Virginia, she wanted to see Florida. Wayne was a graduate student working toward his Ph.D.

Dorothy's brother, Ken, had married Mary Church, on June 22, the year before, and they were living nearby. One evening, Dorothy's parents took Morgan and Erik out to pizza, and the rest of us went to the Oyster Bar for a seafood dinner. After several rounds of beer and dozens of raw oysters, Mary announced that she and Ken were going to Germany in the fall to spend two weeks with her parents, Harris and Mary Church. Harris, commonly called Church, was retiring from a career in the U.S. Air Force and a career in Civil Service. The Churches lived in Ehlenz, a village near Bitburg in the Eifel region. We had met the Churches at Christmas, and really liked them. Ken and Mary asked Dorothy and me if we wanted to join them on their trip to Germany.

At first we said no, even though we both wanted to go. I could work out the time because my dissertation would be finished, but we had two sons, ages nine and seven, who would be in school. There was also the question of money. We had bought a house the year before, and with an instructor's salary, had no reserve funds.

Kathy and Wayne quickly spoke up and said that if we could solve the money problem, they would take care of Morgan and Erik. Like most graduate students, their budget was tight, and they had been living in a rented trailer which Kathy had dubbed "the Hovel." They wanted to spend a few weeks living in a new house, and they also were thinking about having a child of their own when Wayne finished his degree. Our kids really liked both of them, so we were comfortable with their offer, but finances would be a problem. We ended the evening with no decision.

With Mary and Ken's invitation fresh in our mind, and with the reassurance that Kathy and Wayne's offer to help was genuine, Dorothy set about solving our cash problem when we returned to Blacksburg. We had friends in the Accounting Department, who told Dorothy about a way to finance the trip and minimize credit card interest payments. It was all new to us because we had never had a credit card. It involved having two credit cards, neither of which charged interest to borrow cash, and borrowing them back and forth until the debt was paid off. The practice was both legal at the time, and a practical solution to the problem. Credit card companies finally realized that they had a problem and started charging interest to borrow cash. The two cards that we obtained were our first credit cards. We no longer were a cash-and-carry couple.

With the major problems solved, we talked with Morgan and Erik to make sure that they were comfortable with our being away. They assured us that they would be OK. We then asked Mary to confirm her invitation with the Churches, and gave Kathy and Wayne multiple chances to renege on taking care of the boys. They never did.

Cost was still a problem in October 1973, but with cheap tickets on Icelandic Air, we began our journey in October. We started our trip by driving to Watchung, New Jersey, and spent the night with a friend of Dorothy's mother. The next day they took us to Kennedy Airport for our all-night flight to Luxembourg, where we were met by the Churches. Thirty minutes after we flew in, Ken and Mary arrived on Air Bahama.

After arriving in Ehlenz, we were treated to my first Bitburger Pils, a local brew, and took a nap. I had not slept on the plane.

Mary's parents were wonderful hosts for the two weeks that we spent with them. Both were fun to be around and they welcomed Dorothy and me into their family like long lost children. They plied us with good food, lots of wine and beer and without reservation shared their comfortable home with us. Church loaned Ken a car to let us explore the countryside and we took frequent short trips and a few long ones.

The first long trip involved taking their old Mercedes and a very small caravan to Bavaria where we camped in the only campsite that was still open in October. After sightseeing all day, the four of us would return to our home in the campground. The caravan had obviously been built for two midgets, but was now home for three people that were six feet or taller, and Mary, who was the only one of us who could stand up straight in the camper.

The weather was cold, and there was two feet of snow on the ground. Upon returning to the campsite each day, Ken lit the propane heater, and Dorothy and Mary went inside to prepare the evening meal. Lunches out was almost entirely bratwurst on a bun and beer, or Taggessuppe, so we were always starved for a complete meal. The quarters were tight, and Dorothy had to hunker over while they prepared our dinner.

Not wanting to be in their way, Ken and I graciously took lawn chairs from the trunk of the car and pushed them down in the snow, where we sat drinking beer until we were called in for supper.

When it was time to take a bath, we trudged up to an unheated public bathhouse and put in twenty Pfennigs to get warm water. We soon learned that the amount of hot water that you got for twenty Pfennigs was not much, and was inconsistent, thereby leaving you to rinse off in cold water. One experience was enough to make sure that you brought extra money the next time.

Fed, bathed, and wearing multiple layers of clothing, we turned in. Dorothy and I slept in our sleeping bags on the table, after the bench seats were raised to be level with the table-top. With the tight space, we were the first to begin the process of preparing for sleep. We had to spoon one another because our legs were too long to stretch out. If one of us needed to turn over, the other was required to follow suit.

Mary was next. She slept under the table. Her space was so tight that Dorothy had to lean over and zip up her sleeping bag when she was finally nestled in. Finally, Ken would go outside and turn off the propane heater because we were afraid that we might die of carbon monoxide poisoning. He then turned out the light and slept on a much too narrow bench, that otherwise served as a place to sit.

And then someone would have to pee, and we would have to start all over again.

Every morning when we woke up, the inside of the windows were iced over from the moisture in our breath.

When we left Bavaria we headed toward Zurich. On the way through Austria, Ken asked me to look for a shortcut on the map because the route that we were taking would require an additional night on the road. I quickly located one and told him to turn right at the next road.

It was a nice two-lane asphalt road going up the mountain for several miles, before it turned into a two-lane gravel road. A short time later, it became a one lane gravel road in a forest, and then finally turned into dirt ruts in an alpine meadow. Arriving at the top of the mountain, we were met by an Austrian Border Agent in a tiny office who seemed happy that someone had come this way. After a brief conversation and an inquiry into our country of origin, he examined our passports and let us pass. Fifty feet away, we were greeted by the Swiss Border Agent who also checked our credentials and wished us well. As we went down the other side of the mountain, I wondered how many people they saw in a week.

That night we stopped in a village outside of Zurich because the map showed a nearby campground. The map was unclear about which of two roads led to the campsite, and it was already dark. We decided to ask for directions at a restaurant on the edge of the village. Mary was the only one of us that spoke German, but she was tired of carrying the entire communication load and asked me to go in and see if someone spoke English. Once inside, I asked the waiter who was busy serving food, if he spoke our language. In broken English, he said that he did not, but because he understood the question, I was sure that he spoke some. I stood there looking to see if there was another waiter that I could ask. After several minutes, the waiter returned and said that the owner spoke good English, but was cooking someone's dinner. I was told to wait. In a few minutes the owner came from the kitchen and introduced himself as Herr Kohler.

Before I left Blacksburg, a colleague from Hungary, Dr. Michael Kostarab, had advised me to introduce myself by my title, if I ever needed help in Europe. He told me that the degree means more in European society than it does in America. I heeded his advice and replied "Hello, I'm Dr. Allen." It was the only time in my life that I have introduced myself using my title, and it worked. Suddenly, the atmosphere changed. Herr Kohler and I began talking and he asked where I was from and what we were doing in his village. When I explained that I was a Professor at Virginia Tech and a native Floridian, his eyes grew warmer, with the sense that one gets when they meet an old friend. When he found out that I grew up in Kissimmee, he really got excited. He explained that Disney World was a vacation destination for his family every few years.

Now that we knew each other better, he told me that unfortunately the camp ground was closed and that the police would arrest us if we camped there. I followed up with an inquiry about hotels in the village, and he said that there were none. Discouraged with the news, I thanked him and turned to leave. Before I got to the door he said, "Wait a minute Dr. Allen. How long were you planning to stay?"

I responded "Just the night."

"Let me make a phone call."

I listened as Herr Kohler made his call. I could not understand the conversation but could recognize that the call was to the police. When he finished, he told me that we could stay in the parking lot behind his restaurant, as long as we were out by ten o' clock the next morning. He would leave the back door to his upstairs apartment unlocked, so that we could use the facilities. We were so tired that I could have hugged him.

We parked the camper in the back corner of the parking lot and went in to say thanks by eating supper at the restaurant. After being in the cold for most of the trip, the warmth in the restaurant felt good. Most tables were full, but we were given a good table surrounded by people who were enjoying a night out on the town. Beer and wine were flowing and after several days of camp food, the smell of German cooking was intoxicating. We ordered zwei grosse bier for Ken and me, and zwei haus wein for our wives. On the menu we each chose the most expensive entree, wiener schnitzel. The food was delicious, the wine and beer were perfect, and the hospitality that was shown to us by Herr Kohler was something that none of us will ever forget. We both invited him to our homes if he should ever travel near us. He never did.

After seeing a bit of Zurich and taking a tram to the top of the snow-covered Zugspitze, we returned home to Ehlenz for a few days rest. It had been an exhilarating trip.

Our next trip was to Paris. Church loaned us his old Volkswagen Beetle for the trip, because we were not pulling the caravan. Dorothy and Mary got the back seat in the bug and Dorothy rode all the way to Paris with her legs hung over my shoulders.

Mary had found each couple a room at the Hotel Serious for ten dollars a night. The price was squarely in the middle of both our budgets. The hotel was on a side street, three blocks from the Arc de Triomphe on the Champs-Elysees. After we stayed there a few days, we concluded that it might have had a clientele for purposes other than overnight sleeping.

In the city, we walked for miles each day, seeing the sights, and absorbing the culture. Mary had been there before, so was familiar with the city and its charm. I marveled at how she guided us to all the important things to see and do. We saw the Mona Lisa at the Louvre and sat on the steps of the famous Basicila Sacre-Coeur, overlooking the city at night. We walked the left bank of the Seine River and were inspired by Notre-Dame. The four of us visited outdoor markets which sold flowers, vegetables and live birds but mostly we walked and admired the atmosphere. Meals were a reflection of our prosperity, and some of them were taken on the edge of one of our beds with a cheap bottle of wine. As we finished our walk one evening, Mary and I were designated to buy a bottle of wine within our budget. After careful review, we chose the most memorable bottle in any of our past experiences, Vin de Roche, Wine of the Rocks. A Tunisian vintage, it was the cheapest bottle in the shop. That night with the four of us sitting on the edge of our bed, we anxiously opened it. It tasted so terrible that no one took more than a sip. We poured it out and have often laughed about our mistake.

The trips were at times uncomfortable, but through it all we had fun every day, and kept our sense of humor about our living conditions when we were away from the Churches' welcoming home. It was easy because we were young and adventurous.

While we were away, an oil embargo was placed on the USA and its allies' by the OPEC nations to protest the allies support for Israel. Fortunately our friends in Watchung had gassed up the car for us. Their thoughtfulness allowed us to leave with some assurance that we would get partway home. We could only hope that we might find open gas stations. Every time that the gauge showed half full, I started stopping at the next station. Most were out of gasoline, but you could occasionally find one that was still open. We must have stopped at thirty stations, most of which were empty. When we finally got to Christiansburg, Dorothy and I were delighted to be home with our boys. It had been our first trip to Europe, but it would not be our last.

CHAPTER THIRTY-FOUR

THE ENTOMOLOGICAL SOCIETY
OF AMERICA

When I first became a faculty member at VPI in 1968, I rejoined the Entomological Society of America (ESA). The society sponsors a national meeting for the purpose of sharing research findings, teaching curricula, extension and regulatory program methodology among its members. Within the Society there are also five geographical branches, each of which holds an annual ESA branch meeting for the same purpose. For most of my career, the membership was between seven and nine thousand scientists from America and around the world.

As I earlier said, my first experience with the ESA began when I was a student at Purdue University. The national meeting was held in St. Louis, Missouri, in December 1963. I was excited to be attending but nervous about leaving Dorothy, who was a couple of months away from delivering our first baby.

The meeting was presided over by Dr. E.A. Steinhaus, considered by most to be the Father of Insect Pathology. Dr. Steinhaus pioneered work at the University of California, Berkley, using bacteria and viruses to control damaging insects. Bacillus thuringiensis, commonly known as BT in the organic gardening world, was spurred by his early work. His talk was mesmerizing to this young aspiring scientist who knew little of the subject. I left the meeting deeply impressed with what I had experienced, and knew that someday I wanted to be the President of the Society. It was a completely unrealistic goal, but I was too young and naive to know that.

After arriving at VPI, I started attending branch meetings on an annual basis to learn from and discuss progress on my research with other scientists. I began presenting papers, and publishing journal articles related to my Ph.D. dissertation, and my work with soybeans and other insect projects. The more that I got involved with the Society the more I wanted to participate. The interaction with other entomologists broadened my knowledge of Entomology and I made friends beyond my departmental colleagues. I soon became involved with committee work at the branch and national levels. In 1975, I was elected for a three-year term to be Secretary-Treasurer for the 1600 member Eastern Branch of the Entomological Society of America, and in 1983-4, I served as Branch President.

The 1984 Branch meeting was held at the beautiful Hotel Hershey in Hershey, Pennsylvania. I invited Dr. Norman Borlaug, winner of the 1970 Nobel Peace Prize to be the headline speaker for the plenary session. His work as lead scientist in improving wheat production in third world countries was sometimes referred to as the "Green Revolution." Dr. Borlaug had helped millions of the world's poorest people avoid going to bed hungry every night. He and his talk were inspiring, and I was thrilled that he had accepted my invitation.

At the national level, I was elected to represent the Eastern Branch and Section F on the Governing Board for two, three-year terms, and by 1985-6, I had the good fortune to be elected President of the National Society. That year was one of the best years of my career.

The National Meeting was held December 7-11, 1986 at the Bally's Grand Hotel in Reno, Nevada. It was the largest meeting in the history of the ESA, with more than twenty five hundred scientists attending and presenting more than thirteen hundred papers.

I was fortunate that two very capable friends accepted major roles in organizing the meetings. Dr. Gerald (Skip) Jubb had been the Program Chair at the Hershey meeting in 1984 and was my top choice to assume this role at the national level. Program Chair is a huge responsibility for anyone, and to do it for such a large meeting is a major burden. When I called, I expected him to say no, but to my great joy, he accepted. I celebrated that night by drinking an extra glass of wine with Dorothy.

For a meeting that size, the second most difficult Chairmanship is the Local Arrangements Committee. The chair of this committee needed to provide the authors of thirteen hundred papers with slide projectors, screens, and assorted props to keep speakers on time. I turned to Dr. Dick Rice from the University of California. Dick, like Skip and I, had been Branch Secretary-Treasurers, and was experienced at putting on large scientific meetings. I was prepared to be turned down, and once again, was surprised to have Dick accept as soon as I asked. I knew immediately that the meeting was going to be a success.

Now I had only to find a plenary speaker that could inspire enough members to swell the meetings attendance. My choice was one of the world's most famous insect ecologists, Sir T.R.E. Southwood from Scotland. Dr. Southwood had been knighted by Queen Elizabeth for his research accomplishments, and was immediately a big draw for the meeting.

With the program now in good hands, I turned my energy to solving the budget shortage that the Governing Board and the Past President had left for me. Each incoming President is presented with a budget prepared by the previous Governing Board and President. The previous board passed a budget that was almost sixty thousand dollars over the anticipated revenues from dues, publications and meeting attendance.

My next task was to try to get a majority of the 9400 members to significantly raise their dues. Entomologists are notorious for being frugal, and the chance for success seemed doomed at the start. Dues had not been raised for many years. I began by making an appeal to the membership in the ESA Newsletter, and stated the problem as clearly as I could. Several board members wished me luck, but I could tell that they had very little faith that I would get a pro vote. I followed up with a second appeal in the next newsletter. When the votes came in, there were enough pro votes to carry the day. The members had said yes to higher dues. The Executive Director of the Society, Darryl Hansen, and I were relieved. If the Society had voted no, he would have had to fire staff. We now could meet our obligations and plan for a surplus.

The surplus soon dissipated. I received a call from Dr. Donald Duckworth, who had been President in 1983, and who now served as head of the Bishop Museum in Hawaii. Don asked me if I wanted to buy the Journal of Medical Entomology for the ESA. The journal had always been published by the museum and was the premier journal of its kind in the world. Buying the journal would fill a publication void for the Medical and Veterinary Entomologists in ESA. The only catch was that Don insisted that we not disclose the negotiation to anyone. I was caught between transparency and purchasing a publication that would serve seven hundred members of the society. I told him that I could not act without the Boards approval, but would approach the Board and require them to keep our discussions confidential.

In a specially called phone meeting, I laid out my dilemma. Dr. Fred Knapp, from Kentucky, was equally compromised by the need for secrecy, because he represented that section of the society. Everyone on the Board recognized the advantage of making the purchase. There had been rumors that a group of ESA members had approached the museum about purchasing the journal, with the intent of leaving ESA and forming a new society. The loss of those members would have been a major blow. I was determined to not let that happen.

After an hour-long discussion, I received a unanimous vote to purchase the Journal for $40,000. It remains one of the Society's premier journals and members who were on the verge of leaving remained members of the ESA.

A second project that was ongoing that year was the selection of a new office building for the Society. For many years, ESA had housed the Executive Director and his staff in a building that previously had been a small home in College Park, Maryland. The Society had long ago outgrown the space, as the current membership of 9400 members was the largest in the history of the Society. Previous Presidents had acknowledged that a new building was needed, but had not taken action. I decided that with the passage of the dues referendum, it was time to start making plans.

Once again, I turned to Dr. Skip Jubb, who lived close enough to chair a Search Committee. After looking at multiple properties, the society found one that had a generous amount of space for the staff and our publications operation. It also had enough surplus space to rent to other societies, thereby supplementing the mortgage payments on the property. After getting the Board to approve the purchase, the Executive Director worked with Dr. Bobby Pass from the University of Kentucky, who would succeed me as President, to complete the purchase and secure financing the following year.

The Governing Board had worked overtime that year. It had shown great courage in moving forward with the purchase of the Journal of Medical Entomology and the approval of the purchase of a new building. Most of them had taken part in explaining the need for a dues increase. The Board still had one major task to deal with before my year was up. There was a full slate of business transactions and policy items waiting for us at the national meeting. This meeting usually took three long days to complete. More than a hundred and twenty-five items was the norm for this meeting, and my Presidential year was no exception. For years, the pattern had been for the President to present each item and then lead discussion on the information provided and needed actions by the Board. On such a large agenda, it was impossible for the President to be fully informed, and often no action was taken. Many items were tabled until the next meeting and rolled over year after year. I was determined to change that routine, as I considered it a waste of time.

At the beginning of my year as President, I announced to the Board that each member would be assigned items on the agenda. They were informed that it was their responsibility to work with committee chairs in order to present their assigned agenda items to the Board. They were to make motions, as appropriate and lead discussion to deal with their assigned items. My job would be to move the meeting along using Parliamentary Procedure rules. I insisted that we bring closure to as many items as possible. It was a new approach, but the Board rose to the occasion and we left the incoming President, Dr. Bobby Pass, with a nearly clean slate.

Leaving Bobby with a clean slate was important as it turned out. On the day before the National meeting started, he received a new heart from a hospital in Pittsburgh, Pennsylvania. He had been there for some time waiting for a transplant, and had received it at the last minute. He would survive the transplant surgery, and after six weeks, serve out his year as President. Dr. Pass would continue as Department Head at the University of Kentucky for many years after his surgery.

Bobby had alerted me of his condition a few weeks before the meeting started, and asked me to carry on in his place until he recovered, should a donor heart be found. He felt that I was the best person to continue progress toward the purchase of the new building. Bobby and I had been in step with one another the entire year, so that nothing would be dropped when we made the transition at the end of my year. Shocked at first, I agreed, but only if the President-elect, Dr. Lloyd

Knutson, agreed. Being new to the Board, Lloyd was most gracious and Bobby soon returned to his duties.

That December 1986, twenty-five hundred members attended the National meeting in Reno, Nevada. The revenues supplemented those from the dues increase that the members had passed, and swelled the treasury. Even though we had spent $40,000 for the purchase of the Journal of Medical Entomology, we had turned the $59,000 deficit around and finished the year with almost a $100,000 surplus. President Pass completed the mortgage arrangements for the new building after recovering from his heart transplant and assuming his term as President.

Hundreds of ESA volunteers are necessary to fill all the committees, publish the journals and put on the meetings each year. To be a part of that is what makes the time spent so worthwhile. My year was no different. When I stood to deliver my Presidential Address to the twenty five hundred assembled member scientists, it was a humbling experience. It had taken me almost a year to craft what I wanted to say to them. My comments centered on the need to preserve habitat for all the species of the earth, something important to every entomologist. At the end, they were kind enough to stand and applaud.

At every stop along the way, the members had treated Dorothy and me to the best that they had to offer and we enjoyed being with them. It was obvious that they cared about their branch and section affiliation, as well as their National Society.

On the way home we were bumped to first class. I never knew whether the Executive Director, Darryl Hansen, had arranged that, or if it was just by chance. Upon learning that it was our first time up front, the flight attendants brought lots of wine and served us the first rack of lamb that I had ever eaten. We were tired and giddy from our time at the meeting, but were enjoying the trip home. The wine made us mellow. Flying over the Rockies, Dorothy turned to me and said, "I now know what they mean by flying high."

Later, as Dorothy rested, I turned my thoughts to some of the memorable things that had happened to us that year. 1986 had been one of the best years of my career. I had visited all five branches of the Society and was the first president to attend the national meeting of the Livestock Entomology Society, which was held in Glacier National Park, Montana.

Glacier is one of America's most spectacular parks and the four days that Dorothy and I spent with that group of entomologists was educational and recreational. The planners had scheduled time to see the park. Dorothy and I had rented a car at the airport in Billings and were fully mobile. One afternoon, we decided to take a trip up toward Canada to see more of the beautiful countryside. Our car was brand new with only 16 miles on it when we picked it up at the airport. Along the way, we passed a small village in the park that had a restaurant/gift store, ranger office and a gas station where we filled the car with gas for the trip. Everything was going well for the first twenty miles, when suddenly, the engine stopped. We had not seen any sign of civilization since we had left the gas station. In 1986, cell phones were not common and we were stranded.

Trying to allay Dorothy's concerns, I raised the hood and started to look over the engine. I know very little about engines, but decided to poke around and see if something was loose. Nothing was loose. We decided to wait for someone to pass by, and hope that they would stop and help. Forty minutes later, a pickup truck appeared in the distance and when the truck got closer, the driver stopped to inquire about our problem. After explaining our dilemma, he decided to look under the hood. There was still nothing loose. After a few more minutes, he decided to take us back to the small village where we could get help. The fifty mile round trip was out of his way, but he insisted, and we accepted his gracious offer.

The driver was accompanied by his wife and mother-in law, and they were on their way to fish for trout. Dorothy and I climbed into the back of the truck and he delivered us to the gas station. During our conversation, it was revealed that the family was from Lynchburg, Virginia, and that he was a soldier assigned to a small radar facility nearby. I gave him $20 for the gas that he used and thanked him for his help. It was a reminder that there are many kind people in this country, and this young man was one of them.

Back at the village, we notified the rental company. They had the car towed and repaired the next day. We caught a red, open-air touring car back to the lodge later that day, but not before we met Ralph and Debbie Williams and their children in the restaurant. Ralph had been a Ph.D. student at Virginia Tech, but now was a Professor at Purdue University. We had been friends during their stay in Blacksburg and were glad to see them.

Deciding to take this opportunity to catch up with one another, we began walking on one of the hiking trails leading out of the village. After thirty minutes, we began to encounter an exodus of hikers walking rapidly in the opposite direction. When we inquired why, we were told that there was a grizzly bear just up the trail. On hearing that, Dorothy, Debbie and I turned back. Ralph took the kids and continued down the trail, much to Debbie's dismay. Ralph had always been a lot of fun and a bit wild, while a student at Virginia Tech, and now he wanted the kids to see a grizzly bear. As he and the kids walked away, Debbie called out something that we had heard before "Ralph, this is the dumbest thing that you have ever done." We were glad when they returned safely to the lodge that night.

Dorothy accompanied me on all the branch meetings except the Minneapolis meeting in the dead of winter. Each meeting was fun because we got to experience new places and meet new people. The Southwestern Branch meeting was held jointly with the Mexican Entomological Society in Monterrey,

Mexico that year, and was an especially wonderful experience.

Flying to Monterrey, we had a layover in San Antonio, Texas, on St. Patrick's Day. Our stay could not have been better timed. I chose a hotel on the Riverwalk, where we spent hours enjoying the culture of the city. The Riverwalk is a narrow, tree-lined, man-made canal system in the heart of the downtown area that is home to small restaurants, bars and shops. I had been there once before for a meeting, but it was Dorothy's first visit. She loved it at first sight.

St. Patrick's Day was a special time to be in the city because many of the Catholic Churches were celebrating and raising money, by selling home-prepared food along the canal. It was the first time that either of us had eaten green corn tamales, and we loved them. Stopping occasionally for a Margarita at a cantina, and strolling under the lights, the evening turned into one of our favorite memories.

The next day we arrived in Monterrey and taxied to our hotel in the middle of the city. The Holiday Inn was not what I was expecting. It was a beautiful modern high-rise hotel. The corridors to our rooms were open to the center of the enclosed building and had planters filled with Pothos vines hanging down on every floor. The vines gave the hotel a tropical feel in the middle of a dusty city. Looking over the rail you could see the buffet meals being set up in the lobby and the lounge was also in view. We were delighted with the buffet. There were dozens of choices at meal-time and we learned that high quality Mexican food was wonderful.

On two of the evenings, the Sterling Brothers, who owned a big southwestern pest control chain, invited us to the lounge and treated us to drinks and conversation with other attendees. Live music provided Dorothy and me a chance to dance, and at the end of the evening, we could still hear the music from below, as we lay in bed, still fuzzy from the White Russians that we had learned to drink that night.

On another evening, The President of the Southwestern

Branch took us to a cantina outside of the city. He had traveled over much of the area with his research, and said that it was one of his favorite places to eat. Once we walked through the wooden doors in the high adobe walls, we knew why. The open-air plaza was covered with Mexican tile and there were water fountains and a large fire pit for roasting meat and vegetables. Our host had reserved a table near a small fire pit as there was a chill in the air. Over drinks, roasted cabrito and conversation, we spent a perfectly wonderful evening in the countryside.

Our last evening was spent as the guests of the President of the Mexican Society, at a performance of the Ballet Folklorico de Mexico. She spoke little English and we spoke no Spanish but we managed to really enjoy the evening. The singing, dancing and colorful costumes were the perfect end to the trip.

It had been a good year.

Over the years I had invested hundreds of hours of time with ESA and served on dozens of committees in a voluntary capacity. I enjoyed every minute of the journey. Along the way I met some of the world's great scientists and traveled widely. The Entomological Society of America had provided some of the most memorable times of my life, and I had reached the first of the two goals that I had made, while a student at Purdue. The second goal was yet to be attained.

CHAPTER THIRTY-FIVE

GOAL NUMBER TWO

As the years rolled by at Virginia Tech, I would be granted tenure, promoted to full professor and hired into the College Administration as Assistant Dean and Assistant Director of Virginia Cooperative Extension in July 1983. Four years later, in 1987, I was appointed Associate Dean and Associate Director. The promotions and attendant responsibilities were coming every few years. Finally, by 1992, having gone through the ranks, I realized the second of the two goals that I had made while a student at Purdue: I was appointed Interim Director of Virginia Cooperative Extension. The interim title would later be lifted. With a faculty and staff of nearly eight hundred talented and dedicated Extension workers, it was the biggest responsibility of my life.

I and many other agency heads would be challenged by two Virginia governors, Doug Wilder and George Allen, who were in budget cutting moods. Each of my remaining years began with a proposed 15-20% reduction in funds in the Governor's budget. I had inherited a budget composed mostly of salaries, with little room to maneuver. A cut in funds would have meant firing large numbers of faculty and staff.

Fortunately, Virginia Tech's President, Dr. Jim McComas, made our request for funding restoration the University's top priority the year before, and he never wavered in his support when I took over from Dr. Jim Johnson. My job was to make sure that our clientele and legislators knew the full impact of the proposed budget cuts. I could not ask legislators to restore the budget, but I could let them know that they would lose personnel in their district if the cuts were enacted.

The strength of Cooperative Extension is its field staff, and fortunately our citizens and farm organizations made their support known. I followed up with visits to legislators who had questions, and in the end, more than one hundred legislators signed on to the bills to restore funding each year. Even so, there was always one essential vote needed, the Chairman of the House Appropriations Committee. Without the Chairman's approval, the bill would not go to the floor for a vote.

The Honorable Bob Ball was the chairman during my time and that first year, I had not had a chance to present to him my summary of the expected cuts. I needed to convince him that Virginia Cooperative Extension was worth saving. Ralph Byers, the University's Executive Director of Government Relations, arranged for me to have an audience with Chairman Ball shortly before the legislature was to convene in early 1993. It was an experience that I would never forget.

Ralph escorted Dr. Andy Swiger, Dean of the College of Agriculture and Life Sciences, and me to the Chairman's office in Richmond. I had been in the building several times, talking to State Legislators, all of whom had offices near the Capitol grounds. Most of their offices seemed small. When we got to Chairman Ball's office, I was surprised by its sheer size compared to those of the other legislators. When the secretary told us that we could go in, we entered into a large room that was elegantly furnished. Delegate Ball was a short man behind a very large, polished wooden desk.

"Sit down," he said as he motioned to the arm chairs in front of his desk. Ralph and Andy had agreed that I should be the one making the presentation, so I sat in the middle chair closest to the Chairman. Ralph introduced Andy and me, then turned and asked that I take over. Before I could speak Chairman Ball looked me over and snorted "What do YOU want."

His abruptness put me off guard, but I continued as I had planned. "Chairman Ball, I want to thank you for giving us the time to explain the consequences of the proposed budget cuts. I have been able to share this information with many of the other House members. There are one hundred and twenty members of the House and Senate who have signed on to the bill to restore Extension's funding."

The Chairman interrupted "It don't make a God damn what those other sons of bitches want. It's what I want that counts." Suddenly I was on my heels, knowing that I had made an error in judgment, and wondering if I had just lost my chance to restore funding. I had worked for several months to develop the necessary support and realized that I may have just lost it all in single sentence.

Gathering myself, I started reeling off the information as fast as I could. The chairman listened carefully, and asked occasional questions. I answered each question he asked, but quickly returned to the main points of my presentation. After fifteen minutes, he looked down at his watch, then back at me.

"Well, that's all the time I have for you," he said as he rose to show us out of the room. I had not finished all that I wanted to tell him, but now with his abrupt dismissal, I was sure that I had failed. He came around from his desk to walk us to the door. I had no idea how I would recover from blowing this one chance. As we approached the double doors leading to the outer office, Chairman Ball put his hand in the small of my back, as if to push me out the door. He then said "You don't have anything to worry about," as he closed the door.

It took a minute to comprehend what had just happened. Chairman Ball had just schooled a new administrator in the art of using power. He was right, of course. He alone had the power to approve or dismiss the bill. He just wanted me to know it. I only saw him one more time, but each year he allowed our restoration bills to come to the floor for a vote. He was obviously satisfied with the presentation.

To celebrate, the three of us ate a long lunch at a nearby restaurant. I ordered a beer, I needed one.

Even though I had landed on my feet with Chairman Ball, the new governor, George Allen, continued Governor Doug Wilder's campaign to cut funding. In my second year I would gain another ally in my funding wars. Before I became Director, my job was Associate Director for Extension Programming. I had responsibility for programming in Agriculture, Home Economics, 4-H and Community Resource Development. As part of my work, I was in Richmond at a meeting of the Virginia Turfgrass Association on August 2, 1990. Several hundred members were in attendance and I was there to support our specialists who were heavily involved in putting on the conference. After checking into my room, I went to the hotel bar to have a beer before the main conference dinner and program began.

While standing at the bar enjoying my drink, a man in a red suit approached and stood next to me. He ordered a drink and said, "Well, I guess we are in for it now." I asked him what he was talking about. "They're bombing in Kuwait. We're at war with the Iraqis. I just saw it on the TV." Everyone knew that President George H. W. Bush had been assembling a coalition to push Saddam's forces out of Kuwait, but now it had started. After some small talk he introduced himself. "I'm Jerry Clower. I am supposed to be the entertainment tonight. How do you tell a bunch of jokes when people are dying on both sides tonight?" He of course was right. Before the conflict ended on February 28, 1991, three hundred and eighty three allied soldiers and an estimated 100,000 Iraqis would die.

I had not recognized the famous comedian from Mississippi. He asked me what I did for a living and I told him that I worked for Virginia Cooperative Extension. Suddenly his eyes lit up and he wanted to know more. When I mentioned 4-H he began to recount how his 4-H Agent had changed his life when he was a young boy. We talked until it was time to go into the dining hall. As we reached the double doors, he turned to me and said, "It's been nice meeting you. Thanks for talking with me. I think that I know what to talk about tonight."

When it was time for his part on the program, everyone in the room knew that the bombing had started and it was a somber crowd. Jerry addressed the crowd with the news that he was not feeling very funny that night. No one knew what to expect next. What they got was thirty minutes on the value of 4-H and its development of leadership skills that had lasted him a lifetime. He told us that it was his 4-H Agent that first took him out of his county. They went to see Mississippi State University, and his agent later encouraged him to attend the University. He spoke of the values he had learned from his time in 4-H. It was the finest speech about 4-H that I had ever heard. The members gave him a standing ovation at the end. I don't remember him telling a single joke.

In the summer of 1994, I stopped by the Virginia State Fair in Richmond. A large gathering of agricultural leaders and legislators were at the dinner to hear Governor George Allen speak. He was popular with the group that would be attending.

Arriving early, I was walking through the cattle exhibit when I heard someone call my name. When I turned around, there stood a man in a red suit. It was Jerry Clower. I could not believe that he remembered me. We talked a few minutes and he asked me how we were doing in Extension. I told him that I was now the Director and we were having budget problems. He listened intently, then wished me well and continued his trip through the exhibits. I thought nothing more about it.

That night when the Governor spoke he outlined his budget cuts for Extension and Agricultural Research and his justification for sending them to the legislature. At the end of his talk, the crowd clapped politely. A few legislators were enthusiastically applauding.

When Jerry took the microphone, he was funny as usual and had the crowd belly-laughing and slapping their knees.

Everyone was having fun. Then at the end of his routine he paused, and began to lecture the crowd about not cutting Extension funds. Within five minutes he had put the legislators on the defensive. Governor Allen looked uncomfortable. The crowd roared its approval. The man in the red suit had taken the day. Our funds were restored and we had survived another year. It's good to have friends.

It was never necessary to fire anyone for lack of funds, but holding positions was common practice. Holding positions open when vacancies occurred was the only way to have some operating funds for the faculty and staff. It was not an easy time to be in charge.

Three years flew by and I was pleased to be associated with the hard working and talented members of the field staff, the administrative staff, and the specialists housed in four of the University's colleges. Two state and six district administrators were the core administrative staff that year and there were ten program staff to support agent programming. They were an exceptional group of people, as were the administrators of the four colleges with whom I worked.

Thousands of Virginians volunteered to support our programs. I was constantly traveling the state to speak with client groups, sometimes meeting with four groups a day. I enjoyed thanking them for their partnership with Extension, but the message was always the same: I asked them to support their local Extension program. It was a message that was always well received.

All the while, farmers adopted new technology and 4-H children completed projects, attended camp, and learned leadership skills. Families were strengthened by our home demonstration programs, and community leaders were identified and supported, as they worked to make their communities better.

Early in my budding career, I knew that Cooperative Extension and Entomology were the fields that I wanted to pursue. I was not wrong. Both had lived up to my expectations and I was pleased with my choices, but all things come to an end. After working thirty two years, climbing the mountains of responsibility had taken a toll on me. It was time to retire and let someone else take over the Director's job. In my February 28, 1995 letter to the faculty and staff announcing my resignation, I ended with the following statements: "As I prepare to leave the system, I am asking that you respect my wishes that there be no retirement dinners, receptions or other ceremonies. For over 20 years, I have felt that I wanted to exit as quietly as I entered the system." Newspapers across the state carried the notice of my retirement. One copy of the announcement ran in the Roanoke Times & World News on March 7, 1995

Extension Director's last months tough
By Allison Blake
Staff writer

Bill Allen has known since September that he would retire this summer.

But little did the Director of the Virginia Cooperative Extension Service know what a tough several months his last ones would be.

After years of budget cuts, Extension faced perhaps it's hardest battle yet. In the recently ended General Assembly session, legislators restored $7.3 million that Gov. George Allen wanted to cut from the agency's budget.

Bill Allen has taken Virginia Tech up on its faculty buyout offer. He says the endless budget cuts are not the reason he's leaving.

"It certainly contributed to it," he said. "It made the job less enjoyable than if the stress wasn't there."

"But I want to say I've enjoyed this job tremendously. It's been an aspiration of mine. I think that Virginia Cooperative Extension is truly a wonderful organization."

Bill Allen, who will be 56 when he retires June 30, was appointed director last may after serving 20 months as interim director.

"I've never let the word 'interim' get in my way." said Bill Allen, who listed among his achievements the move toward creating community- based citizen leadership councils to set priorities for local extension offices.

"I have loved it, and I want this organization to remain strong. I want people to support it, and that's where the strain has come from this winter, thinking that we might be in the position of having to dismantle the organization. We haven't had the opportunity to build as much as I would like to have."

But he also said that the support from legislators and Tech administrators has been gratifying.

"Bill Allen's done an incredibly fine job, and we are going to miss him, "said Virginia Tech President Paul Torgersen. "There's no question about that."

In a statement, the dean of Tech's College of Agriculture and Life Sciences called Bill Allen's leadership " brilliant."

"His consensus-building style, his thoughtfulness and consideration of each person in the organization, his determination to reshape programs to meet Virginia's needs- all have served Cooperative Extension, Virginia Tech and the commonwealth exceedingly well," Dean Andy Swiger said.

Bill Allen has worked in extension for 31 years. He came to Tech in 1983 as the universities extension entomologist after spending years as a county extension agent in his native Florida. He also worked for extension in Indiana while studying for his master's degree at Purdue University.

The story had one statement worth correcting, I had arrived on March 1, 1968.

My career ended July 1, 1995. I was fifty-six years old but was ready for a new chapter of my life.

People often asked me how long it took for me to retire. They were surprised by my answer. I had maintained an intense work schedule throughout my career. "Twelve minutes," I told them. "Five minutes to drive home, two minutes to get out of the suit, and five minutes to make the Margaritas." It has been twenty-four years since I retired and unlike some colleagues, I have had no regrets.

CHAPTER THIRTY-SIX

LIFE ON THE ROAD: A TRAVEL ODYSSEY

People asked if I was planning to travel after I retired, and again were surprised by my decision. "Not much," was the standard reply. I had traveled extensively in my career. My survey entomology work had required three days of travel within the state each week from March through October. As my career progressed, so did other travel requirements. By the time that I was Director, Dorothy and my secretary, Diane Bolling, communicated directly with one another to keep me packed and scheduled. Over the years, my travels took me to every county and city in Virginia, and to most of the states in the USA. I had traveled to fifteen countries on business and associated travel, and Dorothy had accompanied me to twelve of them. We also had traveled to another five on vacations and were ready to stay home for a while. I had gone to places that I had only read about, both overseas and in the United States. In 1976, I spent three weeks in Les Cayes, Haiti, in support of Virginia Tech's International Corn Breeding Program. Dr. Gary Rusche was in charge of the project to introduce a high lysine gene into the native corn. His hybridized corn was designed to improve the protein content of native corn, which was a staple in the local diet. Protein deficiency was common in Haitian children, and the protein in the new corn could improve their health. My assignment in Haiti involved trying to control fall armyworm, a year-round pest of most crops in the tropics.

The time that I spent there was my first in a third world

country. The Dictator, Jean-Claude Duvalier, also known as "Baby Doc," ran the country with an iron fist. When we traveled, we had to stop at checkpoints, declare our destination, and show passports. Men with machine guns manned the check points. Because Gary was driving a pick-up truck, the officer in charge would usually require him to take passengers along. On one occasion, when we went to Les Anglais, Gary was given a package and told to see that it was delivered to the addressee. Gary explained that this was common practice and that he had received packages and mail in this fashion. Mail service was inconsistent or non-existent in much of the countryside. We delivered the package to a vendor in a small kiosk that sold sundries. The vendor assured us that he knew the person. The addressee lived in the mountains and came to the village every few weeks. He promised to give it to him on his next visit.

When we went to a village, it was often necessary to first speak to a local leader. The local people often called me "Le Grand Blanc," the Big White. Once, when Gary introduced me to someone, he referred to me as Dr. Allen. The man's eyes widened and he told Gary that he wanted me to come home with him because his mother was sick. When told that I was not that kind of doctor, he wanted to know what kind I was. Gary explained that I studied insects. Again, his eyes widened and he asked "Why would he want to cure the bugs?" He had a point.

Two years later, I returned to Haiti for two weeks but could never find a better regimen of control than the one that was commonly used before I became involved.

My next assignment was Israel. The Israeli invitation came to the University from the Governor's office, and I was chosen by the university to explore their irrigation technology. At the time I was the Program Leader for Agriculture, and the Director, Dr. Mitch Geasler, thought that I was the appropriate choice although I was not an engineer.

Representatives from more than twenty countries had been invited. One bus carried English speaking people and another carried those who spoke Spanish. The English-speaking bus was accompanied by a man called Uzi. We wondered where he got that name but assumed that it had something to do with weaponry. We stayed at kibbutzim and observed a wide variety of Israeli farming practices. The Israelis were masters in desert irrigation, taking water from the Sea of Galilee and redistributing it to every region of the country. Their irrigation was so efficient, that when we traveled north from the Dead Sea, we suddenly came upon a large field of bananas growing in the desert. Each banana plant was fed by a small, plastic drip pipe.

Evening meals at the Kibbutz were provided by our hosts. The menu was nearly always the same, roast chicken and sweet red wine accompanied by vegetables from the farm. The food was very good but after ten days of the same diet everyone was ready for a change of menu.

A Scotsman on our bus surprised us one morning when we boarded after breakfast. The night before, he had drawn chicken cartoons and taped a different cartoon to every window on the bus. Every cartoon was hilarious. Taking the hint, our host provided tilapia for dinner that night. We then returned to a steady diet of roast chicken and sweet red wine. That day was thereafter known on the bus as "The Great Chicken Rebellion."

Security was tight for our trip. When we stopped for a comfort break, there often was a contingent of heavily-armed Israeli soldiers nearby. On our last night before returning to Tel Aviv, we stayed in a small coastal town near the northern border with Lebanon. After dinner I wanted to see the water and to be alone for a while. I left the small hotel where we were staying and walked toward the Mediterranean. There was very little light on the street and I was the only one out walking. As I got near the sea, I suddenly realized that my movements were being carefully monitored from the watchtowers. Realizing that I could be mistaken for a terrorist, I made a hasty retreat. I had been foolish but It was the only time that I felt unsafe on the trip.

Mitch Geasler next decided that I should go to China, with John Wolford, the Department Head in Poultry Science. We were going to evaluate the Chinese poultry industry and would be accompanied by a Taiwanese business man, Dr. Lee, who still owned property in mainland China. Not being trained in modern poultry production, my role was largely to help John, to meet with local officials, and to learn as much as possible.

Our Chinese government host spoke English well, and knew more than we had expected about the United States. On the second day of the trip, we learned that he had studied in Chicago for two years. He was interested in our report because the Chinese wanted to increase their consumption of meat. Our host confided that every person got a ration of one egg each day and a kilo (2.2 pounds) of pork a month. He told us that there were no exceptions.

John and I quickly realized that the Chinese poultry farms were equivalent to those that had operated in the USA during the early 1950s. The modern American poultry industry operated with the use of capital, management and scientific research. The Chinese model relied on labor to keep everyone employed. John was quickly at an impasse to provide useful recommendations. They needed fundamental changes in their management practices.

As we traveled the countryside out of Hangzhou in a minibus, I was astounded by the number of people that we saw each day and by their resourcefulness. Every square inch was planted to vegetables and fruit. Vegetables were planted to within a foot of the houses and canals had plants growing down to the waterline. Inter-planting and multi-cropping were everywhere. Geese weeded some of the crops. On the poultry farms, dead chickens were not buried or burned like American farmers often do, they instead were fed to fresh water crabs that were in ponds on the farm. The crabs were then harvested and eaten. On two occasions the crabs were served to John and me with our meal.

Everywhere we went, the people were friendly. We met mayors, business leaders, farm managers, and laborers toiling at their job. At a tea farm we ate on a table from the fourteenth century. It had been well used and it was easy to imagine all of the generations that had taken a meal on it.

When once we had a flat tire in a small village, our driver asked us to get out of the bus so that he could make the repair. While we waited by the side of the road a crowd of children gathered, and then adults started joining them. John and I realized that we were probably the only Caucasians that they had ever seen. Both of us were over six feet tall, with blond complexions and white hair. Only a few of the men were taller than our shoulders. I have often wondered what their conversations were like at their evening meal.

On the last night in Hangzhou, John, Dr. Lee and I were treated to a farewell dinner at a famous restaurant on West Lake. We ate in a small room that was said to be where Chiang Kai-shek had eaten his last meal before leaving China. On the walls were paintings from the last emperor's brother. From the time that we had arrived in China, I had requested that they tell me what was on the menu. I had eaten everything that was served and enjoyed it. That night, they said that they would tell me when we returned to the hotel. In the process of saying good-bye it never came up. I suspect that it was dog. Earlier in the trip I had taken pictures of a dog's carcass being prepared for eating. It did not taste like chicken!

A few days after we first arrived, I had come down with pneumonia, which was with me the entire trip. Although I carried through with my assignment, I finally needed medical attention near the end of the trip. Our host arranged for me to be treated by a medical professional who examined me and gave me a dozen capsules for treatment. The box that the medicine was packaged in had Chinese and English language instructions. The ingredients were Snake Bile and Honey. I took most of them with no relief and brought the last few home for my physician, Dr. Charley Boatwright. We both had a good laugh.

My odyssey continued during the summer of 1985 when the Kellogg Foundation sponsored a Leadership Development Tour to Europe. Five states, five European countries and a USDA representative were selected for the information exchange. Each state got two representatives, and I was fortunate to be one of those chosen by the Director to represent Virginia. The purpose of the trip was to share with one another how we were coping with program development in a downsizing budget climate. Spouses were invited, but paid their way from their family budget. I asked Dorothy to accompany me.

The Director, Mitch Geasler, chose England and Finland for his two countries and I traveled to Sweden and Ireland. Ireland was our first stop. Extension was making major changes in that country, moving toward supporting bed and breakfast tourism. The number of positions was being reduced and the agent's geographical area was being expanded. Ireland's dilemma was a forerunner to what was soon to happen in this country. Evenings were spent at someone's farmhouse eating salmon. Unlike my time in Israel, no one ever suggested any other menu. Flags of Ireland and the USA were displayed on the tables to make us feel welcome and we did.

On the last night in Dublin, our host invited us to a Ceilidh in the basement of her apartment building. Dorothy and I, and another couple, accepted her invitation.

The huge apartment building's basement was divided into four rooms. As you entered through the barroom you were immediately struck by the number of people that were there.

Ages ranged from very young children to old men and women with gnarled fingers and white hair. Guinness flowed from kegs behind the bar and the floor was wet in spots from spilled beverage. People were loudly talking and laughing at one another's stories.

In an adjacent room, old men and teens played musical instruments in groups that formed spontaneously and later broke apart. No one seemed to care whether or not those just learning played perfectly. The whole point of that concert seemed to be to teach the old tunes to the next generation.

In the third and largest room a band played and there was lively dancing by young and old. Hardly anyone sat out a dance. Many of them came over to meet these strangers, and everyone made us feel right at home. It was all spontaneous. Once Dorothy and I found the Guinness and the dance floor, I never bothered to find out what was happening in the fourth room. Late that night, our host took two very tired, but happy people, back to our hotel. It had been a wonderful end to our time in Ireland.

In Sweden, our host took us to very modern farms, one of which raised pigs that had been genetically modified to supply heart valves and other body parts for use in human surgery. A day of fun also was built into the schedule, with a boat trip to a Viking archaeological site on an island and time to see a part of the city of Uppsala. A Scandanavian meal of gravlox at a riverside restaurant was a special treat. Dorothy and I loved the meal and received portions from those who had less adventurous appetites. Our host was happy to see someone who truly appreciated gravlox. Trips through the countryside revealed fields of rape seed (canola) in full bloom. The yellow flowers against a cobalt blue sky took your breath away. In Uppsala, we were housed in the former home of the famous botanist, Carolus Linnaeus. The home had been converted into a small hotel. It was easy to imagine that Linnaeus might have planted the gardens himself.

At the end of a week in each country, all of the representatives gathered in Copenhagen, Denmark, to present their final report and share their experiences. The first day of the meeting brought a surprise. Arriving at eight o'clock in the morning, each participant found a shot glass at their place and a bottle of Gammel Dansk on the table. The first order of business, once the meeting started, was to have a toast. I had never had spirits at that time of the day, but thought to myself that the Danes were on to something. So, I had another. Later in the day, when some of the discussion dragged, I considered having a third but thought better of it.

The last evening in Copenhagen, we were taken to dinner at a restaurant in a restored village. Cocktails, good food and conversation preceded the evening's after dinner entertainment. Expecting a speaker, we were delighted to learn that there was none. Instead, our host passed out sheet music to familiar American songs and we all sang for almost an hour. It was a delightful way to end our trip.

Once that the Kellogg trip was over, Dorothy and I extended our time in Europe by taking the ferry over to Kristiansand, Norway to meet some of Dorothy's relatives. Her Norwegian grandparents were from Kristiansand and Arendal. The relatives had been warned that we were coming, and we were met at the dock by the entire family. That night Ingaborg Myklebust prepared a wonderful dinner for our Norwegian family to welcome Dorothy and me. Ingaborg had four grown daughters, Hildegunn, Ingrid, Eirin and Margareth which were Dorothy's second cousins, and she had invited other relatives into her home to meet us. Hildegunn loaned us her apartment for a place to stay.

Ingaborg and the older family members had vivid memories of Dorothy's grandparent's Gunwald Langeland and Gunda Knutsen. Dorothy's father, Arthur, also had visited the relatives in 1930 when he was 15 years old. Knowing that we were coming, Margareth's husband, Gitle Helland took

Dorothy and me to see the farm that Gunwald's father had sold before moving to Kristiansand. A bachelor lived in the farm house and showed us around the farm but declined to allow us in the house. He did show us where he hid his valuables under the barn during the Nazi occupation. Based on the pictures that we had, the farm had not changed much since Gunwald had lived there.

Dorothy's Norwegian family proved to be wonderful hosts and Kristiansand now holds a special memory for us. At the airport, on our way home, we were surprised by a gift from Gitle. He handed us a reindeer pelt from one that he killed the year before. It has been hung in a prominent place in our home for the last thirty two years.

In 1990, a few years after our initial visit, we took Morgan and Erik over to meet their Norwegian relatives and to see some of their ancestral home. Traveling by train, we crossed the mountains from Oslo to Sognefjord where we took the ferry to a small village on the fjord. A boarding house had been recommended by a Norwegian faculty member at Virginia Tech. That night Morgan went to bed early, but Dorothy, Erik and I opened a bottle of "Virginia Gentleman" whiskey and sat on our balcony and watched the sun set on a mountain at midnight. After a side trip to see a glacier, we took the ferry to Bergen and later flew to Kristiansand. Our Norwegian family graciously hosted us once again.

The next year, the five states in the exchange would host representatives from the five countries who had generously shared their time and programs with us.

The Extension Director, Mitch Geasler, left the university in 1989 and was replaced by Dr. Jim Johnson. In the spring of 1992, while Dorothy and I were preparing to go to Hawaii for our thirtieth anniversary, I received a call from Jim asking me to stop by his office. When I arrived, he told me that the governor was authorizing a trip to Russia, Belarus and Ukraine and that the university had a seat on the trip. The Berlin Wall had fallen on November 9, 1989, and over the next few years, the Soviet Union was disintegrating. Ordinary citizens were experiencing freedom for the first time in their lives. The Governor had asked the Commissioner of the Department of Agriculture and Consumer Services, Dr. Clint Turner, to put together a group of people to see if there were business opportunities in the rapidly changing landscape. Jim told me that he wanted me to go and represent Virginia Tech.

At first I told Jim that I did not want to go because the dates of the trip conflicted with our June 17 anniversary plans. He persisted, and I eventually acquiesced, with the caveat that I could bring Dorothy at my expense.

We arrived in St. Petersburg, Russia, dead tired, and suffering from jet lag from the overnight trip. We were expecting to be taken to our hotel so that we might rest, but instead our Russian host loaded everyone up on a bus for a visit to the State Hermitage Museum. Russia's incredible museum of art is the second largest in the world. We were allowed only two hours to see the exhibits, but could have spent days wandering the halls looking at paintings and artifacts that are considered to be among the world's finest. Tired and hungry, we were finally taken to the Pribaltiyskaya Hotel on the shores of the Gulf of Finland for dinner and a much needed night's sleep.

A few days after arriving, we celebrated our thirtieth wedding anniversary on June 17, 1992. We were surprised by a dinner and dance that was attended by the American Consulate to Russia, who sat at our table. A special cake had been ordered to commemorate the occasion, and with lots of wine and a live band for dancing, the evening was one to remember. Then it was back to our room, where we slept in small single beds. They had not thought of everything!

Bill and Dorothy Allen celebrating their thirtieth wedding anniversary at the Pribaltiyskaya Hotel in St. Petersburg, Russia - June 17, 1992.

The next two weeks were spent looking at collective farms, meeting with scientists, businessmen and government bureaucrats. Everyone was enjoying their new-found freedom of speech. People were candid with their responses to our questions, and often began their talks with, "If I had told you what I am about to say a few years ago, I would have been shot."

Visits to their collective farms always began with our farm host providing us with bread and salt. It was an old Russian tradition. The noonday meals on the farms were served home style at long tables. At every meal that we ate in Russia, there were bottles of vodka on the table and toasting was expected. The Commissioner and I seemed to do most of the toasts. On my earlier trip to China, I had performed this same function at the evening meals with the traditional charge to everyone to "Ganbei," the Chinese version of "Bottoms Up."

Unless requested, there usually was no drinking water. Everyone was expected to buy bottled water at the then exorbitant prices of five dollars for two liters. We were told that most Russians earned less than twenty dollars a month in 1992.

Most of the farms were operating very inefficiently. Large inventories of farm equipment lay rusting, for want of parts to repair them. We were told that it was easier to buy new equipment than to try to find parts. Unlike farms in western countries where the farmer performs all of the farm chores, there was a division of labor where workers usually only performed one task. The inefficiency was mind boggling. Our host relayed that the farm workers had been offered the chance to leave the collective and be granted a piece of land for their house and farm, but few had the courage to accept. They did not know enough of the total farm operation to start their own farm.

After leaving St. Petersburg, we flew to Kiev, Ukraine, and stayed at a small hotel near the sports stadium. The stadium was said to have been a part of the 1980 Olympic Games. Arriving hot and tired in the afternoon, we were shown to our room on the third floor. A short stout woman in a Soviet style uniform was stationed at a desk in the hallway. When you left your room, she collected your key, and kept it until you returned. There was no air conditioning in our room and the June weather in Kiev was hot. When I asked about finding a cold beer, a maid assured me that she could get us one, right away. On subsequent evenings, she had cold beer waiting for us when we returned at the end of the day. The room had a garden view and our stay was pleasant.

On Sunday afternoon we walked to the stadium and were surprised that there was a flea market selling used household items. Many of the vendors had little to sell and one of them was selling a single shoe. They were struggling to make ends meet.

A trip to a farmer's market was an opposite experience to that we had seen at the stadium. Fruits, vegetables, herbs and meat were plentiful. People were buying fresh produce and looked happy and well fed. Strawberries were in season, and Dorothy purchased a large bag of the sweet red berries for snacking. They were among the best that I had ever eaten.

By the end of our time in Ukraine, we had learned that the people did not care for the Russians. Stalin had starved millions of Ukrainians during his reign as he collectivized their farms, and they had not forgotten.

Our next stop was in Minsk, Belarus, a country where Nazis had slaughtered thousands of civilians during the Second World War. Walking away from the hotel one afternoon, Dorothy and I stopped in a grocery store. We were shocked at how little food was for sale. The only thing that was not in short supply were large jars of beets that had been on the shelf so long that they were covered with a thick layer of dust. When we walked back to the hotel, we met an old man fishing on a bridge over a waterway. Without either of us speaking a common language, we used hand gestures to discuss the day's catch, which had been meager. The language of fishing is the same all over the world.

The trip ended in Moscow where we stayed at a very modern French hotel that was associated with an ophthalmological surgical institute. We were ready for some upscale accommodations and French cuisine. In the course of a few days we saw a lot of the city on the way to our appointments. On one occasion we went to the Kremlin, where upon entering, we were told to line up against the wall. Nervous laughter and comments preceded the suggestion that this might be our last day in Russia. When our time came, we were ushered into the basement of the Kremlin and shown the vestments of past royalty. That same day we walked through Red Square and near the tomb of Lenin. Five years earlier I could never have imagined that Dorothy and I would be walking in the capitol of Russia. It was a heady time in our lives.

As we were strolling through Red Square, our guide shared the news that there was fighting in two of the former countries that composed the former USSR, and that soldiers had been called out to quell an uprising in Moscow. They were going through a turbulent time and we sensed our guide's unease.

By the end of our trip, the group concluded that the thing the Russians needed in 1992 was paint for all of the wonderful architecture that had been neglected for the previous seventy-five years. We saw little opportunity for agriculture but I did suggest that they needed a Cooperative Extension Service.

After the usual round of meetings, the trip ended with a party at another hotel. The beautiful dining area was in the basement of the building, but half-windows looked out onto the street. Wine and good food was served and violin music was being played. Many of us danced, and we discussed what we had learned. Although we were being treated to a wonderful party, Dorothy and I both felt strange. Bureaucrats and their guests were having a wonderful time eating, drinking and dancing while the eye level view of the streets revealed people who were struggling to make ends meet. Some were begging, and others were hustling anything that they could sell. The Russians were reworking a political and economic system that was all that they had ever known. Everything was on shaky ground, and their future was still up in the air.

CHAPTER THIRTY-SEVEN

SUNSETS

Once I retired, Dorothy and I bought a house in Florida to escape the Blacksburg winters, and became snowbirds. After a four year stay in Bonita Springs, we sold that house, and built a home in Palm Coast. The community that we now live in is perfect for us. Our property abuts a seven-acre retention pond, with a wetland preserve on the other side of the water. The wetlands attract a wide variety of wildlife, and there are daily wildlife sightings from our house and lanai. Alligators cruise the pond, and we see ospreys and a variety of shore birds, and turtles. Otters visit periodically, and eagles can be spotted, soaring high in the cobalt blue sky.

An hour before dinner, I pour Dorothy and me a glass of wine, and we sit and talk on our bench at the ponds edge, watching the sun reflect the bay magnolias and pines on the surface of the water. The scene changes enough each day to inspire us with the beauty of nature. Our neighbors sometime join us to talk and laugh until it's time to go inside for dinner.

Ten years ago two friends and I stocked the pond with largemouth bass so now twenty minutes in the back yard usually provides enough catch-and-release fishing entertainment for those of us who like to fish. The beach is only fifteen minutes away and there are 28 parks and 150 miles of walking and bike trails in our small county. We have come to love Flagler County as much as we love Blacksburg.

Dorothy's family lives nearby and we see them a few times each year. Her brother, Dr. Ken Langeland, and his wife Mary live in Gainesville, and we occasionally see their daughters, Zoee and Nellie, with their spouses and children.

We continue to travel occasionally, but the trips are fewer and strictly for pleasure. Three weeks in Greece, two weeks in Switzerland, a week in Jamaica, and two weeks in Italy are highlights. For our fiftieth wedding anniversary, we went to the Mayan Coast of Mexico and spent the day with a group of twenty-year olds, zip lining and jumping from a high platform into a cenote. Snorkeling to the end of a cave, we had our anniversary picture taken sitting on a rock with snorkels and masks on our head. These days, with lower energy, we realize that we may soon become cruise candidates.

Eighty years now have passed since I was born on June 15, 1939, and I am in the twilight of my life. I realize what a fortunate and amazing life that I have led. Dorothy and I are still reasonably healthy, and I love her as much as the day we married on June 17, 1962. We have raised two sons who are successful professionals. Both are married and are good husbands and fathers. Morgan and Josephine have given us two granddaughters, Samantha and Hanna. They live nearby and we see them often, when we are in Blacksburg. Erik and Claudia are parents to our grandsons, Zack and Luke, who live in Richmond. Although our visits with our Richmond family are less frequent, every visit is an important event in our lives.

From the time of my first memories, I have loved to fish. Mom fostered that passion, and I have never outgrown it. In the winter, I fish from the shore or in my fifty-year old canoe. It is the same canoe that Dorothy's brother, Ken, brought from Sarasota, Florida to Blacksburg, on top of his old VW Beetle, in the spring of 1969. The canoe has seen a lot of time on the water. When the boys were young, I took them down the New River fishing for sunfish, smallmouth bass and goggle-eyes almost every weekend in the summer. We froze our catch and ate fish all winter. Dorothy used the canoe for several years to paddle the rivers near Blacksburg, with a group of faculty wives called the White Water Women. Now she has another canoe, and the original plies the backwater of Pellicer Bay on days when I choose not to fish from the shore.

On those days when I fish alone on the little wooden bridge at Princess Place Preserve, I often reflect on my life and the people who helped shape it. Most of those from my early years are gone now, but I remember them well. Of my siblings, only Jo Marie remains. She lives in Indiana near her daughters. I haven't seen her in more than forty years but we have recently reestablished contact and I am learning what a remarkable woman she turned out to be. Denise died in Tallahassee on September 15, 1999. She had a hard life and died alone. My brother Leon survived three tours in Vietnam, retired from the Army, and settled in Panama City, Florida, to be near his children. Leon passed away on August 19, 2008, eight years after Denise left us. Mike, an aviation mechanic in the Navy for twenty years, retired and lived in Virginia Beach, near the Naval station in his waning years. He left us on June 5, 2013. In my later years I learned that both Denise and Mike experienced periods of substance abuse and homelessness; Denise in Orlando and Mike near the naval base. Nothing came easy for any of them proving once again that the shadows of war are long.

As I wait for my red and white popping cork to disappear beneath the surface of the water, I remember their faces and sometimes when the wind passes through the marsh grasses, I can almost hear their voices. Their words are the milestones of my life. Some words give pleasure and others are haunting.

"OK boys, get your flashlights. It's time to catch some toads."

"Bill, go get Ada. I need her. Tell her that I'm bleeding."

"It's time to eat, get washed up. Bill go fetch some oranges while I fry the hoecakes. Be careful out there in the dark."

"I never thought I would raise a coward. You are a coward. A coward is what you are."

"Bill, you and Trigger get in the skeeter, we're going to the store to cool off."

"Well boy, if you stay here, you may never get so you like it, but you will God damn sure know what work is."

"Bill, are you awake? Your Dad killed himself tonight. I've got to go to the funeral home. Do you want to come?"

"Hey Bill, let's go to college."

"Yes, I will marry you."

"Congratulations Mr. Allen, You have a fine healthy boy and your wife is doing well."

"Dorothy's still asleep, but she's doing fine and your second son is too. He's a long one."

"Good morning Bill, I'm calling to tell you that you have been elected President-Elect of the Entomological Society of America. You will do a great job"

"Congratulations Bill, you are the new Director of Virginia Cooperative Extension."

Standing by the water, their words help me recall the happy days before the war, when Dad played with Leon and me on warm summer evenings, and when he and Mom giggled and laughed as they bathed one another in the dark at the outdoor pump. But the laughing stopped when he went to war and could not control the memories when he returned. I ask myself, why those memories finally drove him to ruin two families, and to kill himself and Iona, leaving their children as orphans. And I can never understand or reconcile it.

In my mind, I replay all the times when Mom worked at the mill and struggled to keep us fed and housed, once in little more than a shack, but always with a roof over our head. She did the best that she could, and in the end found a man that adopted her three youngest children, and stayed with her until her death on April 29, 1976. Although she and Walter were poor as church mice, I hope that they were happy with one another.

And then there's Uncle Leon, who came to our family's

rescue too many times to count, and who took me in when I was fourteen and needed a place to live. He was my benefactor, and served the larger role of moral compass at a time when I needed one. He asked nothing more of me than that I work hard, and that I conduct myself responsibly.

Standing above the outgoing tide as it flows under the bridge, I think of all of the people who aided me in my journey as I grew from being an awkward school boy with no future, to a career in a major university. They were friends, teachers, professors and colleagues that I worked with along my journey. Each had an impact and I am thankful for their part in my life.

But most of all, as I stand by the water reflecting on my life I think about the impact that Dorothy has had. She came along and brought the ambrosia. Suddenly the hoecakes were all behind me and I had finally cast aside the shadows of my father's war experience. The future now was ours to share and we have done just that. For more than a half century, she has supported me, loved me, brought two wonderful sons into our life, and provided the happiness that everyone deserves. Together we have shared a full life.

Then suddenly, the red and white cork disappears, and I stop reflecting and live in the present. A beautiful speckled sea trout has taken the bait, and I know that all is well in the world.

EPILOGUE

War has been a part of mankind's experience throughout recorded history. Animals make war as well. Chimpanzees kill chimps from other troops and sometimes eat their rivals, but only man has developed the ability to create death on an industrial scale.

In my lifetime, upwards of a hundred million people have died in military conflicts around the world, and millions more have been physically injured and/or dislocated from their home. Some, like my father, escape physical harm, but never escape the mental agony from the long shadows of war. The memories are too real, the guilt unbearable.

Armed conflicts cause countries to be ruined, buildings become rubble, crops destroyed, infrastructure is lost and basic humanity degrades into the ash heap of unintended consequences.

I often ask myself what would the world be like if people stopped wasting blood and treasure in pursuit of territory, resources, power, hate and pride. If the nations of the world could find peace, would there be enough for all of us to live comfortably? I believe that there would be. Swords could finally be turned into plowshares and the unleashed talent of our species would transform the world into a better place. Water and air could be cleaner, crop land made more productive, infrastructure made stronger, pandemics diminished, the homeless could be helped and native habitat restored.

It is unlikely that we will see those changes in our lifetime, because the territorial imperative is strong, but one can hope. In 1955, Pete Seeger wrote a hauntingly beautiful anti-war folk song "Where Have All The Flowers Gone?" One line in that song raises a simple but eloquent question, "When will they ever learn, when WILL they ever learn?"

ABOUT THE AUTHOR

The author is a fifth-generation Floridian who grew up in Kissimmee in the nineteen forties and fifties. He is now retired from Virginia Tech where he served in the Department of Entomology for fifteen years, before moving into administration. He retired in 1995 as Director of Virginia Cooperative Extension and Associate Dean of the College of Agriculture and Life Sciences. He has been involved in more than fifty scientific papers and reports, was awarded more than three million dollars in grants, and had an active role in training Graduate Students in the Department of Entomology.

Dr. Allen is an Emeritus Professor at Virginia Tech who has been recognized numerous times for his scientific and educational work on behalf of farmers and other citizens. He served as President of the Entomological Society of America in 1986.

Married to Dorothy Marie (Langeland) Allen, his wife of 57 years, they have two married sons, and four grandchildren.

They are residents of Palm Coast Florida, but they also spend significant time in Blacksburg, Virginia, where they have been a part of the community for 52 years.

This is his first book.

A PARTIAL LIST OF THE ALLEN AND KING FAMILY MEMBERS MENTIONED IN THE BOOK

GREAT, GREAT GRANDPARENTS
    ALLEN FAMILY
        JOHN LANIER, 1805 -1888
        MARGARET HOGANS, 1810 - bef. 1883

GREAT GRANDPARENTS
    ALLEN FAMILY
        WILLIAM ALLEN, 1850 - 1924
        NANCY JANE NIPPER, 1869 - 1941

        COLUMBUS STEPHEN ACREE, 1854 - 1924
        ELIZA T. LANIER, 1859 - 1932

    KING FAMILY
        LORRIN KINGSLEY LOOMIS, 1825 - 1864
        EUNICE ANN MANN, 1829 -1905

        JOHN EMIL PALMQUIST, 1865 - 1938
        MARY ELIZABETH JOHNSON, 1866 - 1931

GRANDPARENTS AND GREAT UNCLE
    ALLEN FAMILY
        WILLIAM HARVEL ALLEN, 1888 - 1967
        RUBY ESTELLE ACREE, 1892 - 1968
        LEON VERNON ALLEN (GREAT UNCLE), 1894 - 1966

KING FAMILY
    ALBERT KINGSLEY LOOMIS (ALBERT L. KING), 1857-
    1941
    HANNAH ELIZABETH SOPHIA PALMQUIST, 1898 -
    1931

CHILDREN OF WILLIAM H. ALLEN AND RUBY E. ACREE
    HARVEL CLIFTON ALLEN, 1913 -1963
    WILLIAM COLUMBUS (W.C.) ALLEN, 1915 - 1973
    IRIS ALLEN, 1916 - 1974
    RALPH CARL ALLEN, 1918 - 1956

ADDITIONAL CHILD OF RUBY ESTELLE ACREE
    RICHARD PERFITT, 1927 - 1969

CHILDREN OF ALBERT L. KING AND HANNAH E. S.
PALMQUIST
    RALPH OBED KING, 1915 - 1990
    EUNICE MARIE KING, 1918 - 1976
    RUTH ELIZABETH KING, 1919 - 2004
    CHARLES CLAIR KING, 1922 - 1981
    ELIZABETH ANN KING, 1925 - 2000
    RICHARD EARL KING, 1928 - LIVING
    VIRGINIA HELEN KING, 1930 - 2010

CHILDREN OF RALPH CARL ALLEN AND EUNICE MARIE
KING
    LEON HARVEL ALLEN, 1936 - 2008
    WILLIAM ALBERT ALLEN (THE AUTHOR) 1939 -
    LIVING
    SANDRA DENISE (ALLEN) ALDERMAN 1947 - 1999

ADDITIONAL CHILDREN OF EUNICE M. KING
      JO MARIE ALDERMAN, - LIVING
      DAVID LEE ALDERMAN, 1953 - 2013

CHILDREN OF RALPH CARL ALLEN AND IONA MAY
ANDREWS,1930 -1956
      RALPH CARL ALLEN JR., 1951 - 2010
      DEE ALLEN
      IRENE ALLEN

CHILDREN OF WILLIAM ALBERT ALLEN AND DOROTHY
MARIE LANGELAND, - LIVING
      MORGAN WILLIAM ALLEN, - LIVING
      ERIK LEON ALLEN, - LIVING

Made in the USA
Columbia, SC
10 May 2020